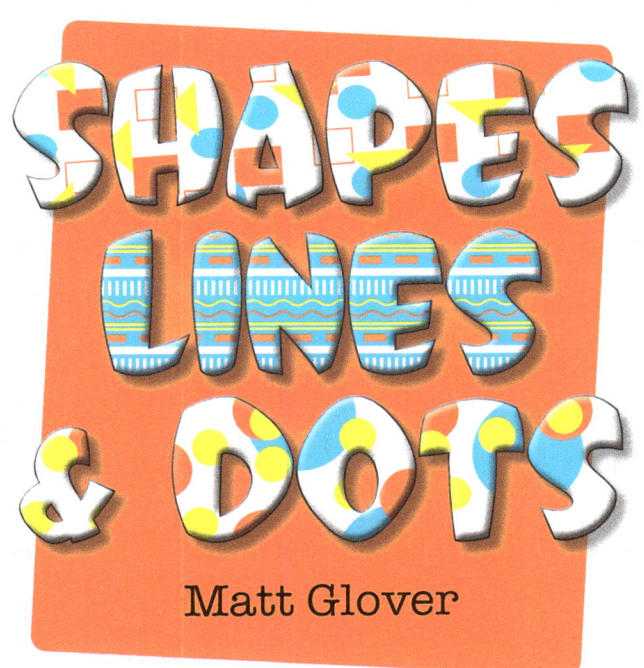

Cartooning, Creativity and Wellbeing for Kids

Shapes, Lines & Dots
September 2016
Published by
MGA Counselling Services Pty Ltd
ISBN: 978-0-9953613-0-0
Words and Images © Matt Glover 2016
www.mattglover.com
Layout and Design by Cara King
www.caratoons.com

A Note for Grown Ups

This is not your typical "how to draw" book for kids.

Shapes, Lines and Dots is about creativity and wellbeing. Being creative has a long list of well documented health benefits. It provides an outlet for emotions, enhances concentration, and improves both stress management and confidence. *Shapes, Lines and Dots* provides an opportunity for your child to explore their creativity and contribute to their own wellbeing at the same time.

Shapes, Lines and Dots also teaches mindful techniques. Mindfulness has been shown to contribute to good mental health in children. The exercises at the end of each chapter include an element of mindfulness, encouraging your child to observe keenly the world around them and record what they see. To get the most out of the mindful elements of this book, ensure all devices are switched off so your child is not distracted from the act of observing and creating.

Shapes, Lines and Dots is not about producing art with a capital 'A' and you don't need to be "artistic" to benefit from this book. It is all about the process of making something that wasn't there before; putting marks on paper and seeing characters come to life. It's fun, it benefits your child, and it's an activity that you can do together.

A Note for Grown Ups

What You Will Need

All you will need to provide is a pencil (HB is fine), some coloured pencils, a pencil sharpener, and a good supply of A4 paper. Don't worry about providing an eraser. In my live workshops I don't let anybody rub anything out - there's no such thing as a mistake in cartoon drawing! If a line ends up somewhere accidently, encourage your child to leave it there and turn it into a creative part of the drawing. In cartoon drawing, circles can have flat bits, wobbly bits, and even corners!!

How it Works

Each drawing is constructed using simple steps, adding shapes and lines and dots in sequence to create over fifty different characters. The drawings get progressively harder as you work through the book, but there are no difficult constructions requiring lightly drawn frameworks or guidelines. Drawings of this nature will be introduced in a future volume.

Encourage your child to attempt the creative/mindful exercises at the end of each chapter. Even better, make some time to do the activities together.

Turn off your phone. Grab a pencil. Let's get creative!

Matt Glover

Matt Glover

Cartooning, Creativity and Wellbeing for Kids

Contents

Welcome	5
Monsters	9
Bugs and Mini-beasts	17
Birds	25
Cats	33
Dogs	41
Sea Creatures	49
Farm Animals	57
Wild Animals	65
People	73
Some Final Words	85

Welcome!

Some people think drawing is hard, but it's not. In fact, if you know how to draw a basic shape, a line and a dot, you already know how to draw cartoons. It really is that simple.

This book shows you how to arrange shapes, lines and dots into different combinations. Before you know it, a cartoon appears before your eyes!

If you've got a grown up reading this to you or sitting nearby, tell them they have to draw something with you. Tell them to stop whatever they are doing because right now, drawing is THE most important thing in the world. Tell them Matt says so!

I'd love to see your work. When you've finished some drawings, choose your favourite and take a photo of it. Then you can email it to me at matt@mattglover.com. Make sure you ask a grown up if you need help.

Ready? Let's draw!

What you will need

Grab a pencil and one for your grown up. Grab lots of paper and make sure a pencil sharpener is handy. You won't need an eraser. In cartooning there is no such thing as a mistake, so if a line goes in a wrong place just leave it there and make it part of the cartoon.

If you want to colour your work in, have some coloured pencils close by too.

Remember we said cartoon drawing was just shapes and lines and dots?

Warm up exercises

Let's do some warm up exercises, filling whole pages with just those things.

Draw a square. Then a rectangle. Then another square. Then another rectangle. Go a little bit crazy and fill the whole page with squares and rectangles. If you don't like squares and rectangles, fill the page with circles, ovals, or triangles. Big ones and small ones. Skinny ones and fat ones. Fill the whole page!

When you've filled the page, colour in some of the spaces. Do it carefully. It will make a pattern that you might like to stick up on your wall. But make sure you leave some wall space for cartoons!!

Now fill up another page with as many lines as you can. Straight lines, waving lines, wiggly and wobbly lines. Spirals and whirls. Zig zags and curves. As many as you can.

Then in random places, place some dots, lots of dots!! It looks cool!!

SHAPES, LINES & DOTS

Now you've shown yourself you can draw shapes, lines and dots, let's use them to draw cartoons.

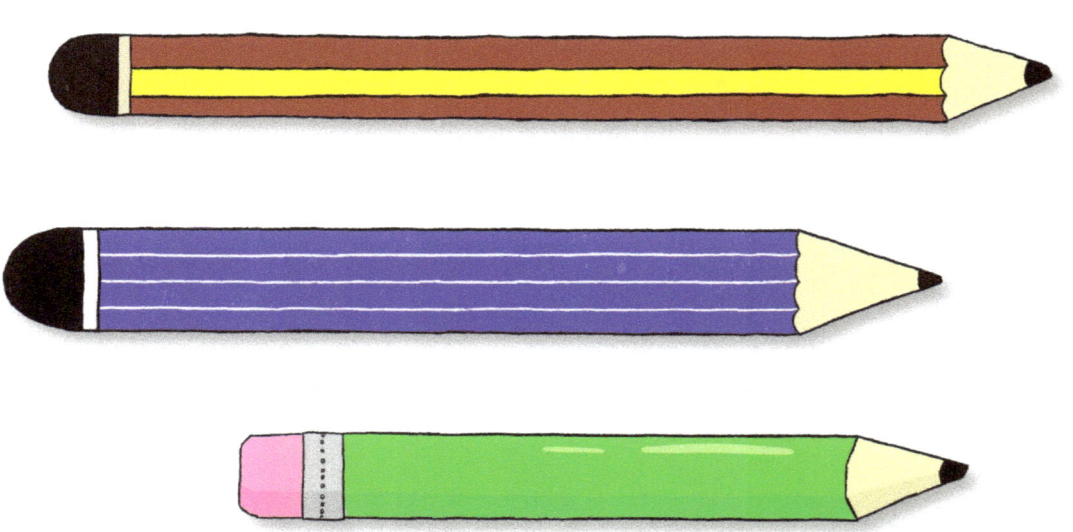

SHAPES, LINES & DOTS

Monsters

Monsters are supposed to be scary, but they're not. They are probably more scared of you than you are of them. A monster once told me he was so scared of little kids that he almost did a little pee in his pants last time he saw one!

Let's start with the simplest and friendliest of all monsters. His name is CT. He will appear from time to time in this book with some great ideas for you to expand your drawing skills even further.

SHAPES, LINES & DOTS

CT Monster

1. Start by drawing an egg shape that is lying on its side.

2. Then draw a circle inside the egg at the fat end.

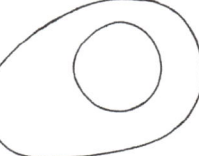

3. Draw a line and a dot like this, to make the eye. Let's add some more lines to make arms and legs for CT.

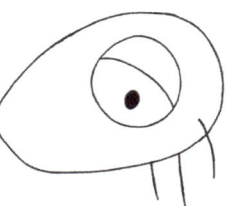

4. On the end of the arm, add four short lines to make simple hands. On the end of the legs, add two ovals to make simple feet.

5. CT is a happy monster. Add a curved line to make him smile, with a small line at the end of the curve to complete the mouth.

6. Add two curved lines for nostrils – CT likes to smell things! Add three lines on top for three strands of hair. Apparently this is the latest trend in monster hairstyles.

7. To finish our drawings, add some colour to CT. Colour him with a green pencil, and choose a slightly darker green for his eyelid.

And before you know it, you've finished your first cartoon! And all you used were *shapes, lines and dots*.

SHAPES, LINES & DOTS

Triangle Monster

This monster is a bit of a nerd. He likes reading Wikipedia and fixing all the incorrect entries. He is very popular in the monster world because he is always willing to share what he knows.

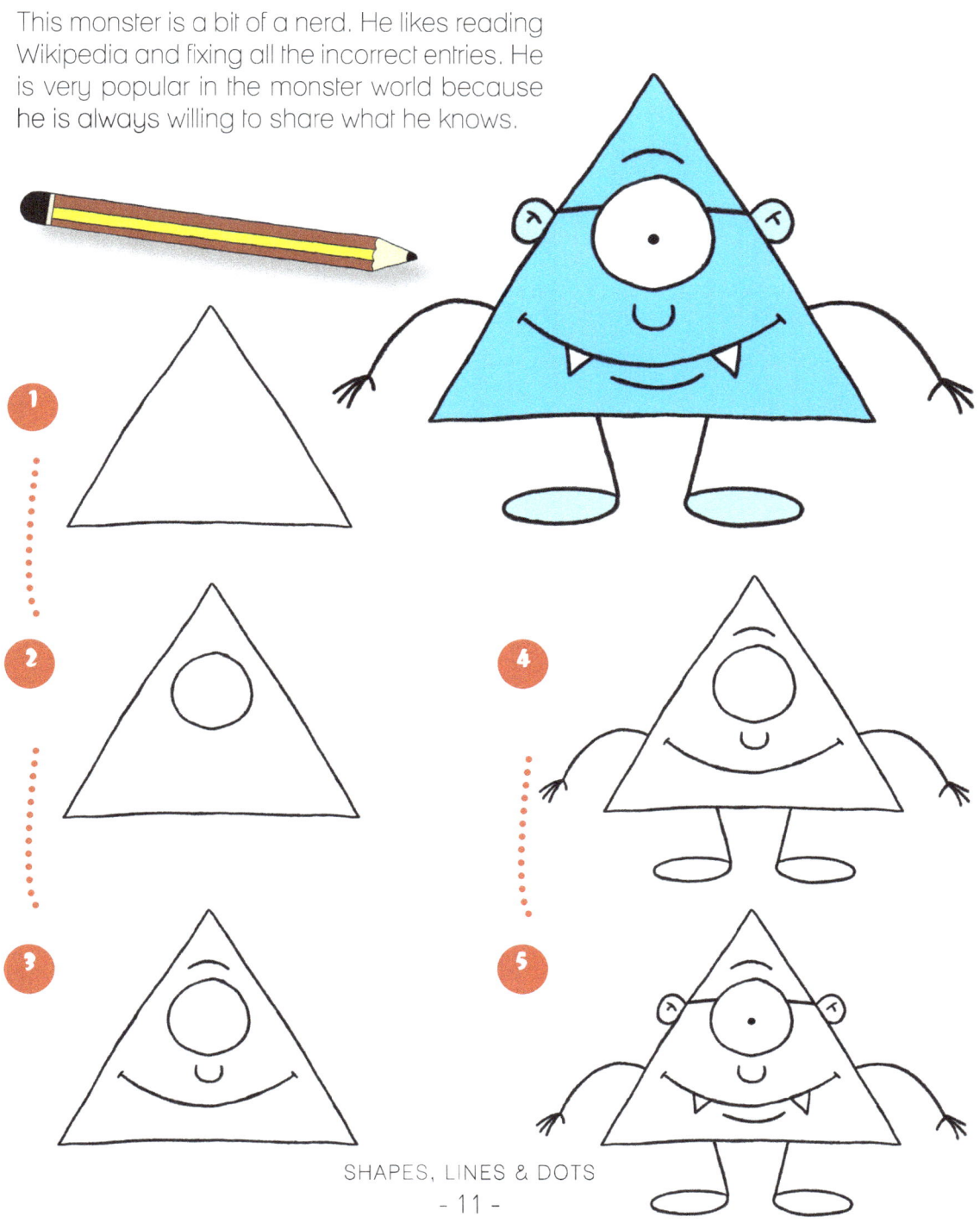

SHAPES, LINES & DOTS

Semi-Circle Monster

Not all monster are boys. This monster is a girl - and she is grumpy! She's grumpy because people keep thinking that all monsters are boys!! She's probably extra grumpy because her teeth are falling out.

1 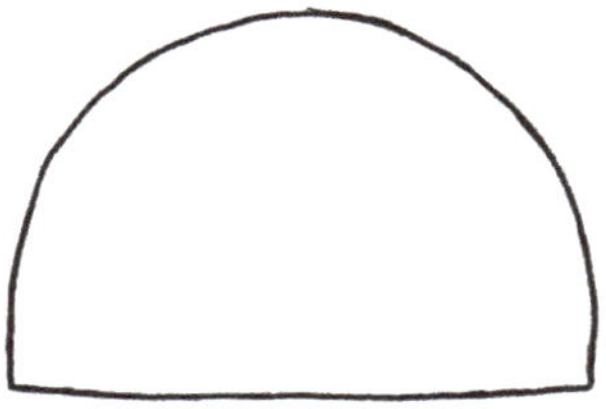
2 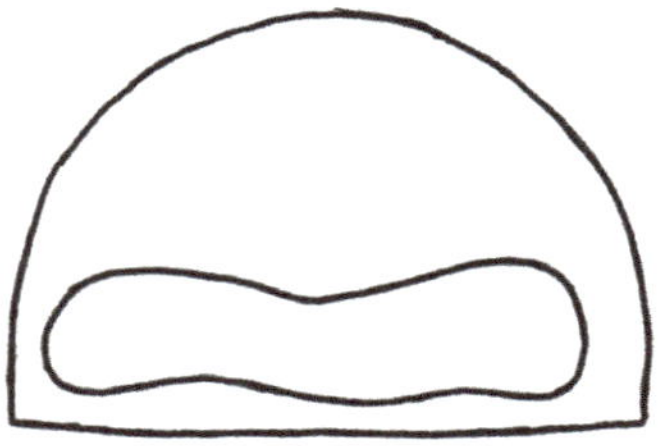
3 
4 
5

SHAPES, LINES & DOTS

- 12 -

Tentacle Monster

It's cool to have six tentacles. It's even cooler to have six tentacles and three eyes. This is one of the happiest monsters you will ever meet, but be warned; if a six tentacle, three eyed monster starts to tickle you, you're a goner!

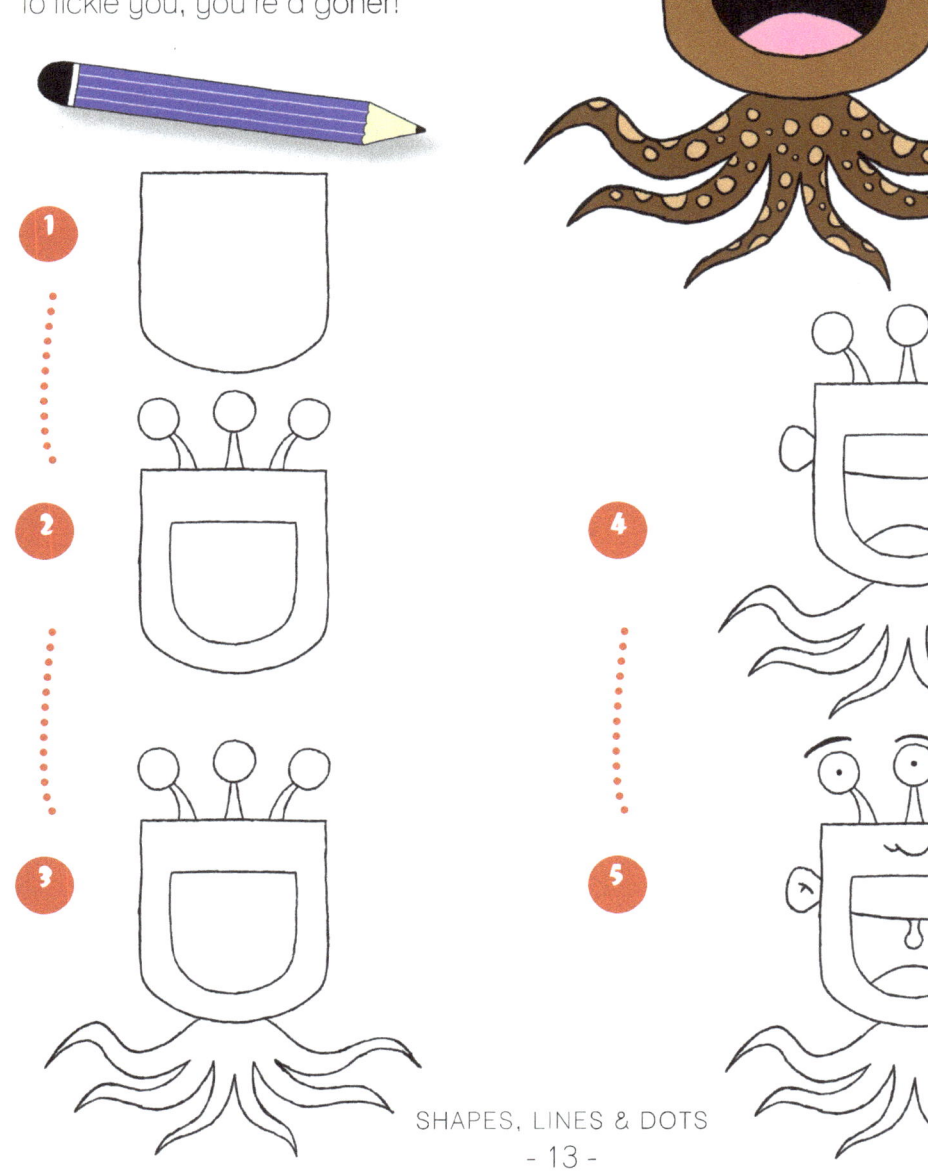

SHAPES, LINES & DOTS

Jeans Monster

This monster likes to wear jeans. A lot. You'll never see this monster wearing anything but blue jeans. Unless, of course, you draw him wearing something else... hint, hint.

SHAPES, LINES & DOTS

Spotty Monster

Spotty Monster is the happiest monster in the world. How could you not be happy with a smile as big as that? Follow the steps to draw the spotty monster and make the smile beam!

1

2

3

4

5

SHAPES, LINES & DOTS

Extra Activities

Turn each of these shapes into monster creations of your own:

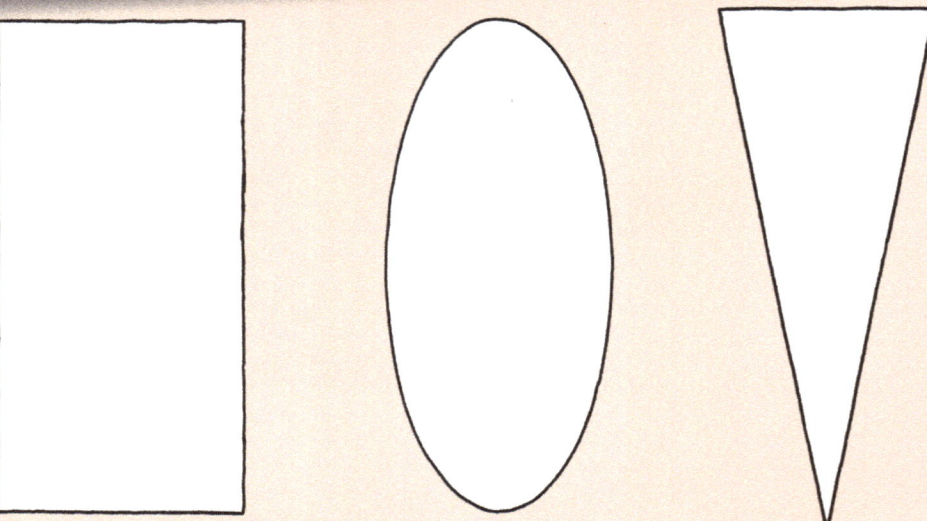

Try some of these extra monster drawing activities:

1. Draw the Semi Circle Monster again, but this time, make her happy. Give her nice teeth too.

2. Draw CT again, and make him look in different directions.

3. Draw the Jeans Monster wearing the same clothes that you are wearing now.

4. Draw a family of Spotty Monsters, making them all a different colour.

SHAPES, LINES & DOTS

Bugs and Mini-beasts

Let's move from monsters to those creepy crawly things that are walking through your garden and flying through your trees. Bugs and mini-beasts are everywhere!

Did you know there are over nine hundred thousand different types of insects living in the world? There are also over thirty-five thousand types of spiders and twenty thousand different types of caterpillars. That's a lot of bugs!

Fortunately, most of them leave us alone. But some of them like to bite. Others are deadly!

Let's draw some of the creatures you might find in your garden. Remember, all we are doing is drawing shapes, lines and dots. But this time we will arrange them so they look like bugs.

SHAPES, LINES & DOTS

Ant

The tiny little bugs that seem to turn up everywhere. Especially when you leave yummy food unattended at a picnic!

This cute ant is simple and fun to draw – follow the steps and then add colour.

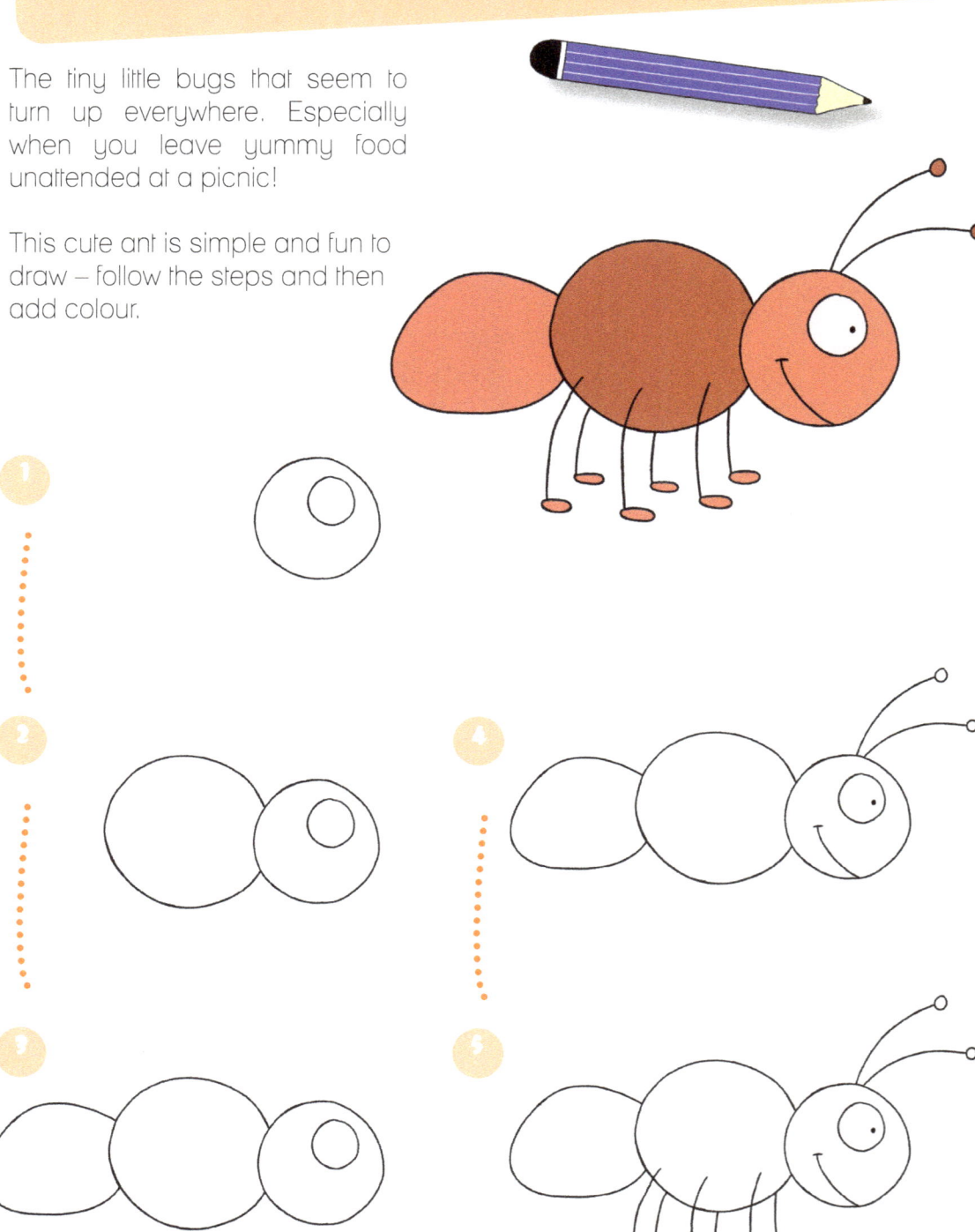

SHAPES, LINES & DOTS

Fly

The most annoying bug of all - the fly. You just can't escape them when it's hot! Humans have one lens in each eye, but did you know that the common house fly has four thousand lenses in each eye?!

1

2

3

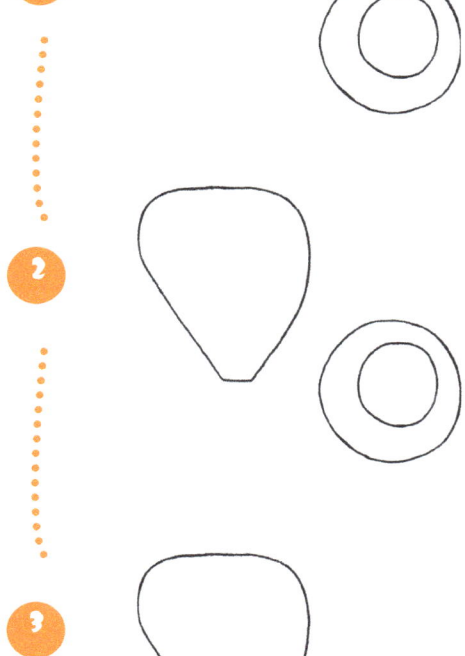

4

5

SHAPES, LINES & DOTS

Bee

Bees make honey - how can you not like bees? Well, apart from the fact that they can sting you, and when they do it really, really hurts! Perhaps it's best if the closest you get to a bee is drawing a cartoon of one.

SHAPES, LINES & DOTS

Mosquito

Here's one that likes to bite. And not only that, it will suck out some of your blood for lunch! If you're going to make friends with a mozzie, make sure it's a boy. Only the girl mozzie bites humans, the boys prefer to eat nectar from flowers.

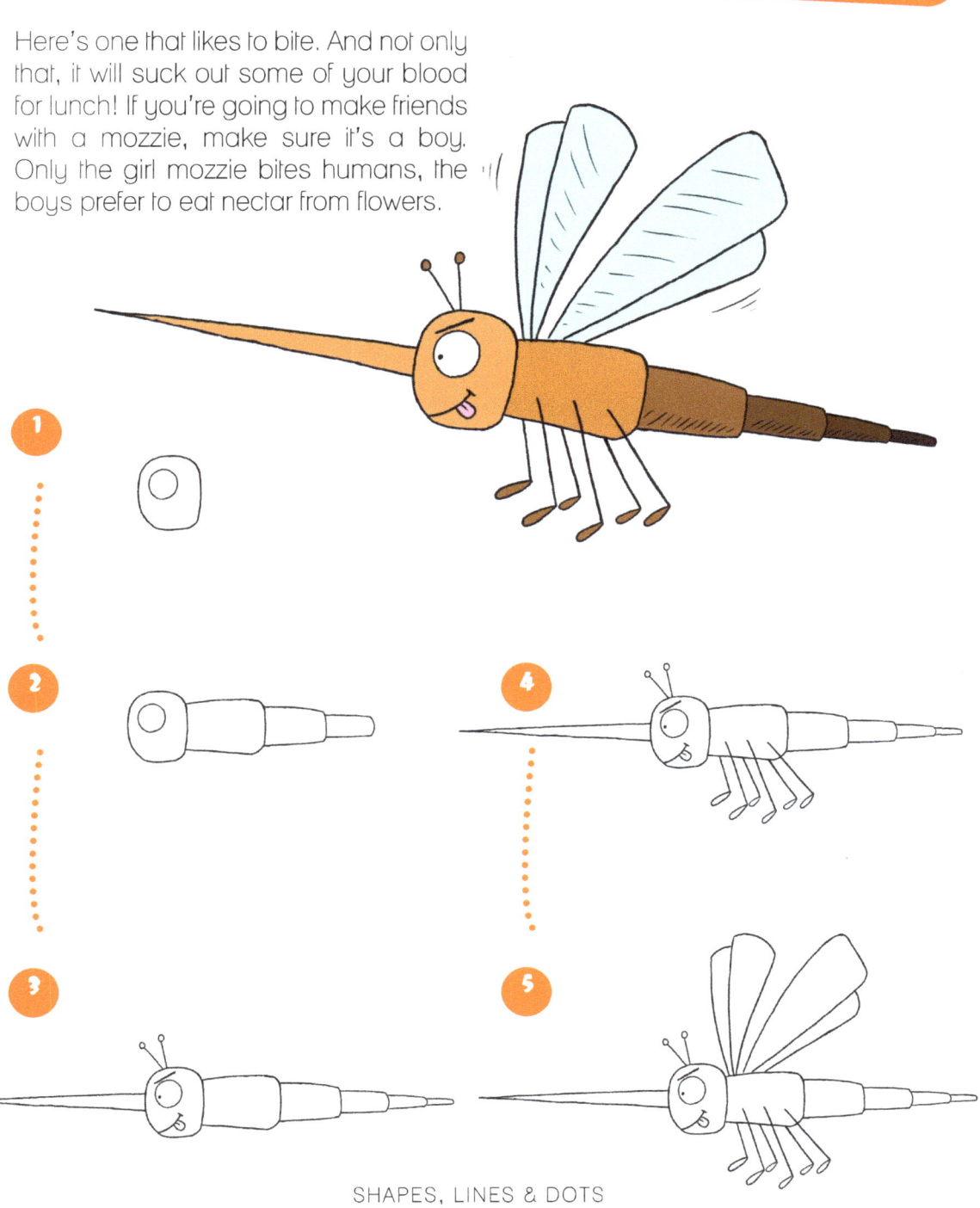

SHAPES, LINES & DOTS

Snail

Have you ever been walking in the garden with bare feet, heard a crunch, and felt something squishy between your toes? You probably stepped on a snail. Some people in other countries like to eat snails for dinner, but I don't recommend you try any of the ones you might find in the garden. An interesting fact – the smallest snail on the planet can fit through the eye of a needle.

SHAPES, LINES & DOTS

Spider

If you're super scared of spiders, you might want to move to Antarctica. They don't have any spiders there! Spiders have eight legs and eight eyes, and can be any colour you can imagine. Some are tiny, but the biggest is the Goliath Birdeater Tarantula which measures 30cm across. Yuk! Fortunately this cartoon spider looks pretty harmless.

SHAPES, LINES & DOTS

Extra Activities

Try some of these extra bug drawing activities!

1. Go outside and see if you can find a non-dangerous bug that we haven't drawn in this book. What shapes make up the body? If it has them, what shape are the wings? How many legs does it have? See if you can draw a cartoon of that bug.

2. Flies sometimes move around in swarms. Draw a whole swarm of flies!

3. What shapes would you use to draw a caterpillar? See if you can draw a caterpillar using shapes, lines and dots. Make it as colourful as you can!

4. Spiders spin webs out of silk. Draw a spider web for your cartoon spider to live in.

5. Do you have a craft box at home? Instead of drawing a bug, see if you can make one out of things in your craft box.

SHAPES, LINES & DOTS

Birds

Birds are beautiful! Sometimes we keep them as pets. Sometimes we feed them in the wild. Other times we hear them singing, even if we don't know where they are.

Some birds fly, but some don't. Some are excellent swimmers while others never go near the water.

They have feathers, wings, lay eggs and are warm blooded. There are over ten thousand different types of birds in the world, but only the hummingbird can fly backwards. Speaking of hummingbirds, the smallest bird in the world is the Bee Hummingbird – it is only 5cm long!

Birds are fun to draw and make great cartoon characters. Use your shapes, lines and dots to draw these cartoon birds!

SHAPES, LINES & DOTS

Chick

The cute little chick is the easiest bird to draw. This chick is trying to fly, but can't get very far off the ground. Make sure you add the small lines that make the wings look like they are moving.

SHAPES, LINES & DOTS

Hungry Bird

This bird looks happy because it is about to have lunch. The worm doesn't look happy because it is about to *be* lunch!

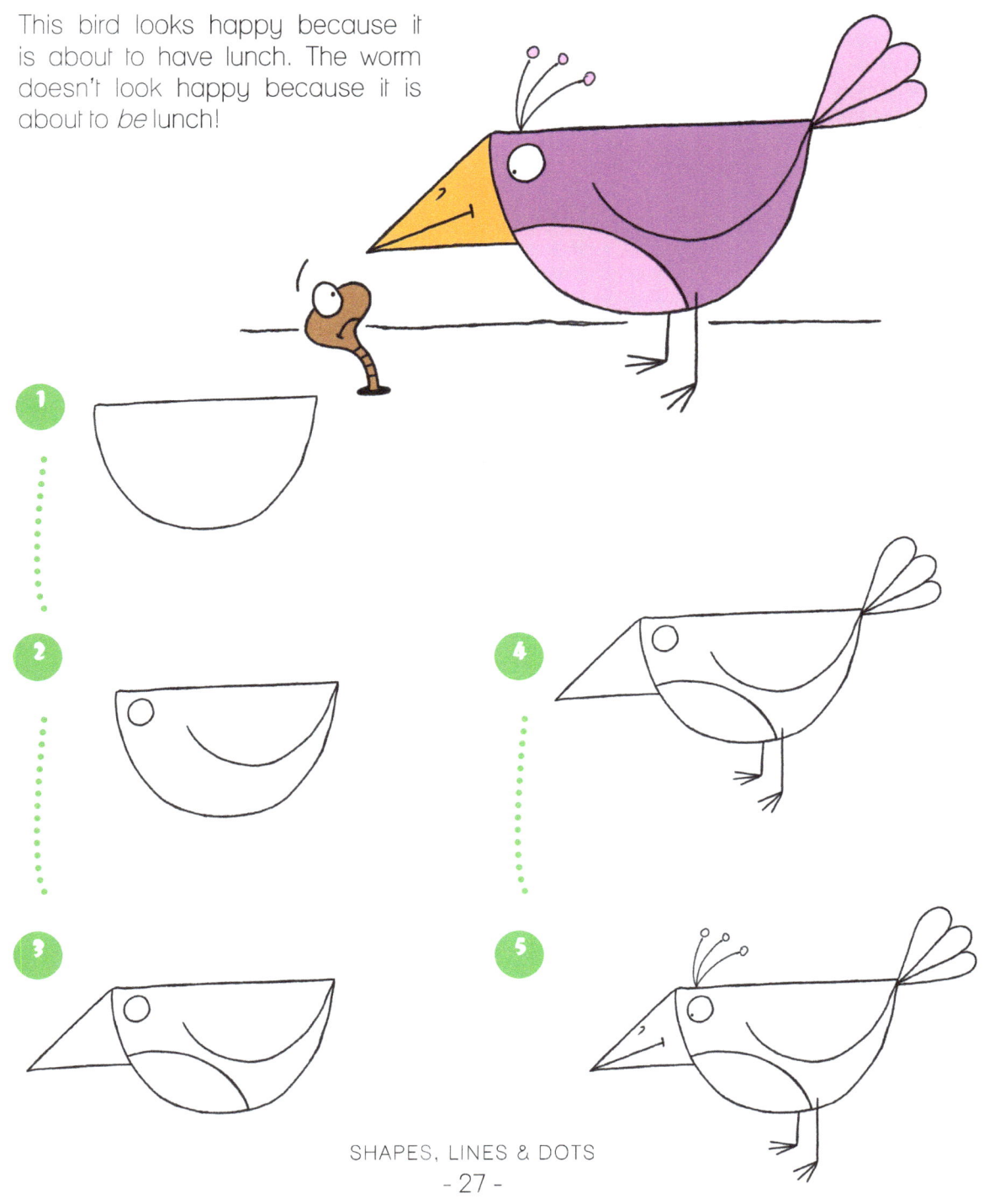

SHAPES, LINES & DOTS

Duck

Have you ever seen ducks swimming on a lake or river and noticed that they never seem to get wet? Follow the steps to draw this duck looking a little surprised!

SHAPES, LINES & DOTS

Flying Bird

There are some birds that fly great distances every year to lay their eggs in a place that is safe and warm. Once the eggs have hatched and the babies are strong enough, they fly all the way back to where they started from. Draw this flying bird using shapes, lines and dots.

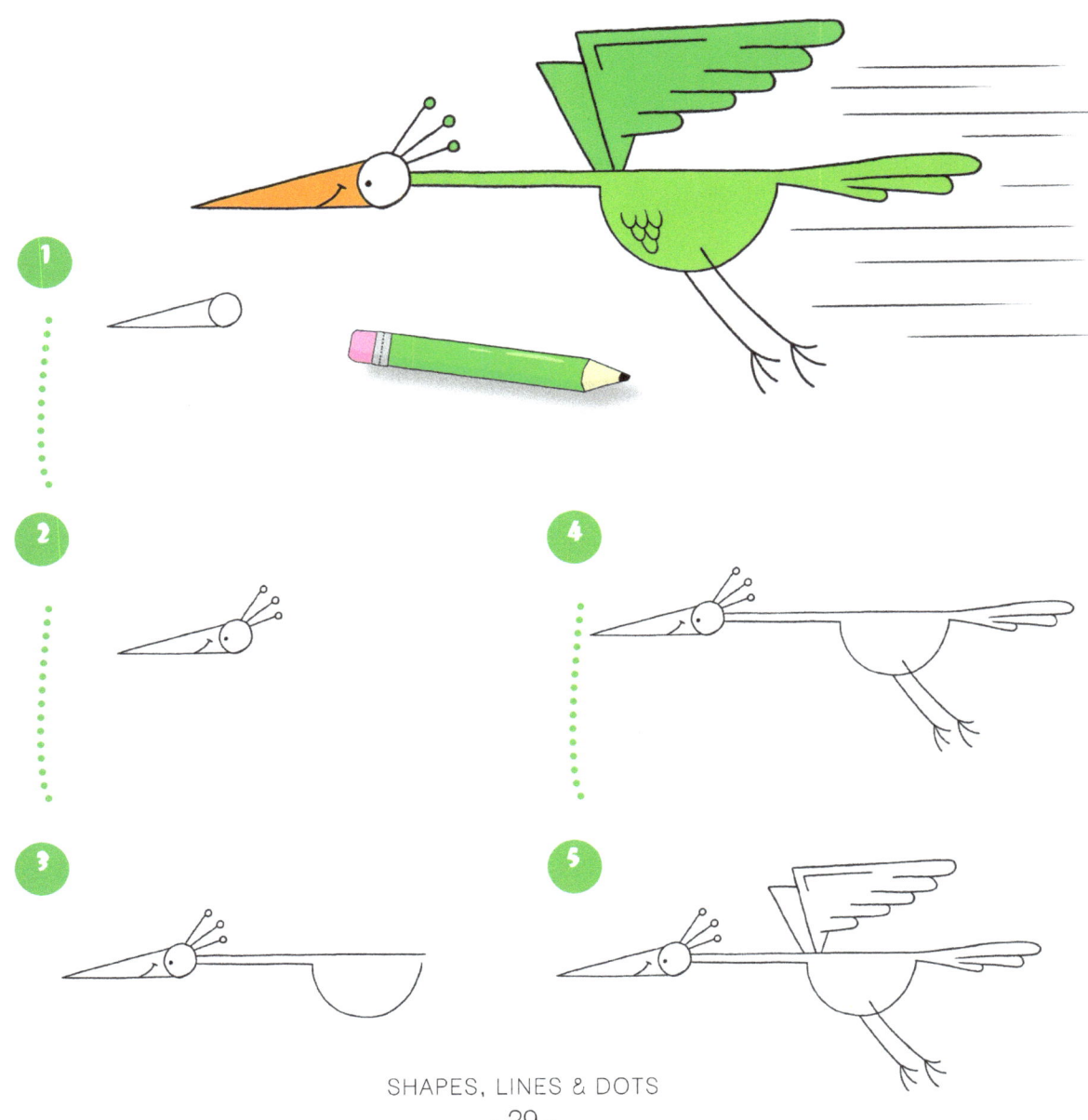

SHAPES, LINES & DOTS

Penguin

This penguin is all dressed up and ready for the **penguin formal**! He can't fly, but he sure knows how to swim quickly to avoid being eaten by seals and sharks. Draw this penguin and then add lots of black to complete his suit.

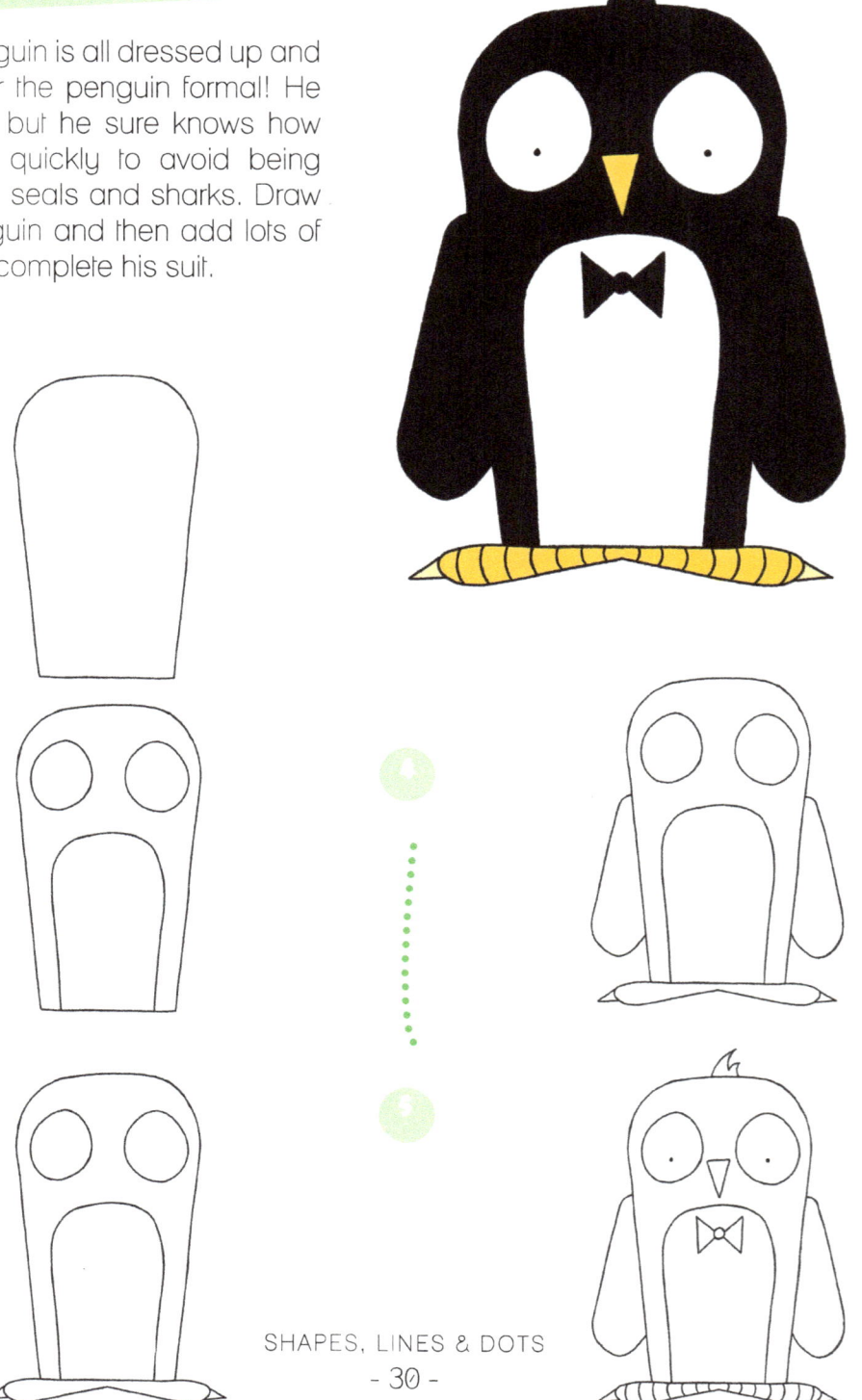

SHAPES, LINES & DOTS

Owl

People sometimes describe owls as being very wise. This owl is still a baby and she hasn't had a chance to learn all she needs to know to become wise. But she always does her homework and hands it in on time – so should you!

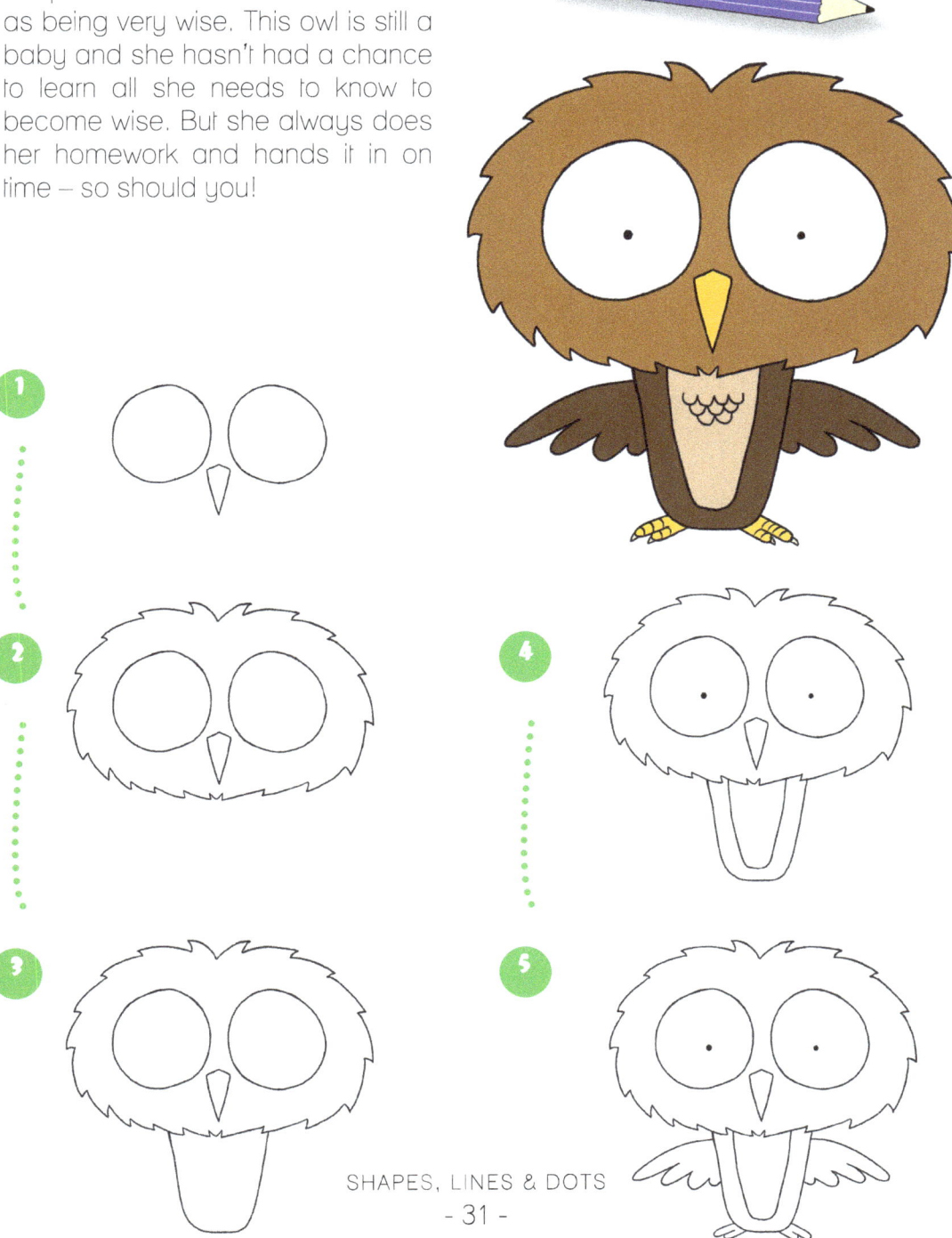

SHAPES, LINES & DOTS

Extra Activities

Try some of these extra bird drawing activities!

1. If you have a pet bird, see if you can draw a picture of it as a cartoon.

2. The dodo was a giant bird that used to live hundreds of years ago but is now extinct. See if you can find a picture of a dodo online and draw a cartoon version of it.

3. Some birds fly in flocks. Take the flying bird cartoon and draw lots of other birds around it to make a flock.

4. Take your paper and pencil outside and sit very still. If a bird comes by, see if you can draw it really quickly. You might need to put some seed, fruit or bread out to attract them.

5. Birds are covered in feathers. See if you can find a feather somewhere and draw it carefully. What shapes, lines and dots can you see?

SHAPES, LINES & DOTS

Cats

I'm allergic to cats. They make my eyes watery and my nose runny. But I also know lots of people love them and have them as pets.

In Australia there are 3.3 million pet cats. That's a lot of runny noses for people like me! However, If I had to choose which animal I would be, a cat is near the top of my list. A cat sleeps 13 to 14 hours a day, which sounds pretty good to me!

Using shapes, lines and dots, let's draw some cats.

SHAPES, LINES & DOTS

Cats on 2 legs

Cartoon cats don't have to do what real cats do. This cartoon feline is quite comfortable walking on two legs like a human.

SHAPES, LINES & DOTS
- 34 -

Cats on 4 legs

Here is the cat from our last drawing, being a bit more cat-like by walking on all four legs. Which version do you prefer?

SHAPES, LINES & DOTS

Fat Cat

Regardless if they are on two legs or four, if they do not exercise they will get fat. This guy is big and round and a slightly odd colour for a cat. This is cartoon drawing and we can make cats any colour we like!

SHAPES, LINES & DOTS

Fluffy Cat

This fluffy cat is a little more difficult to draw. It uses a series of lines to form the shape of the body. Examine it closely then take your time to make it look just right.

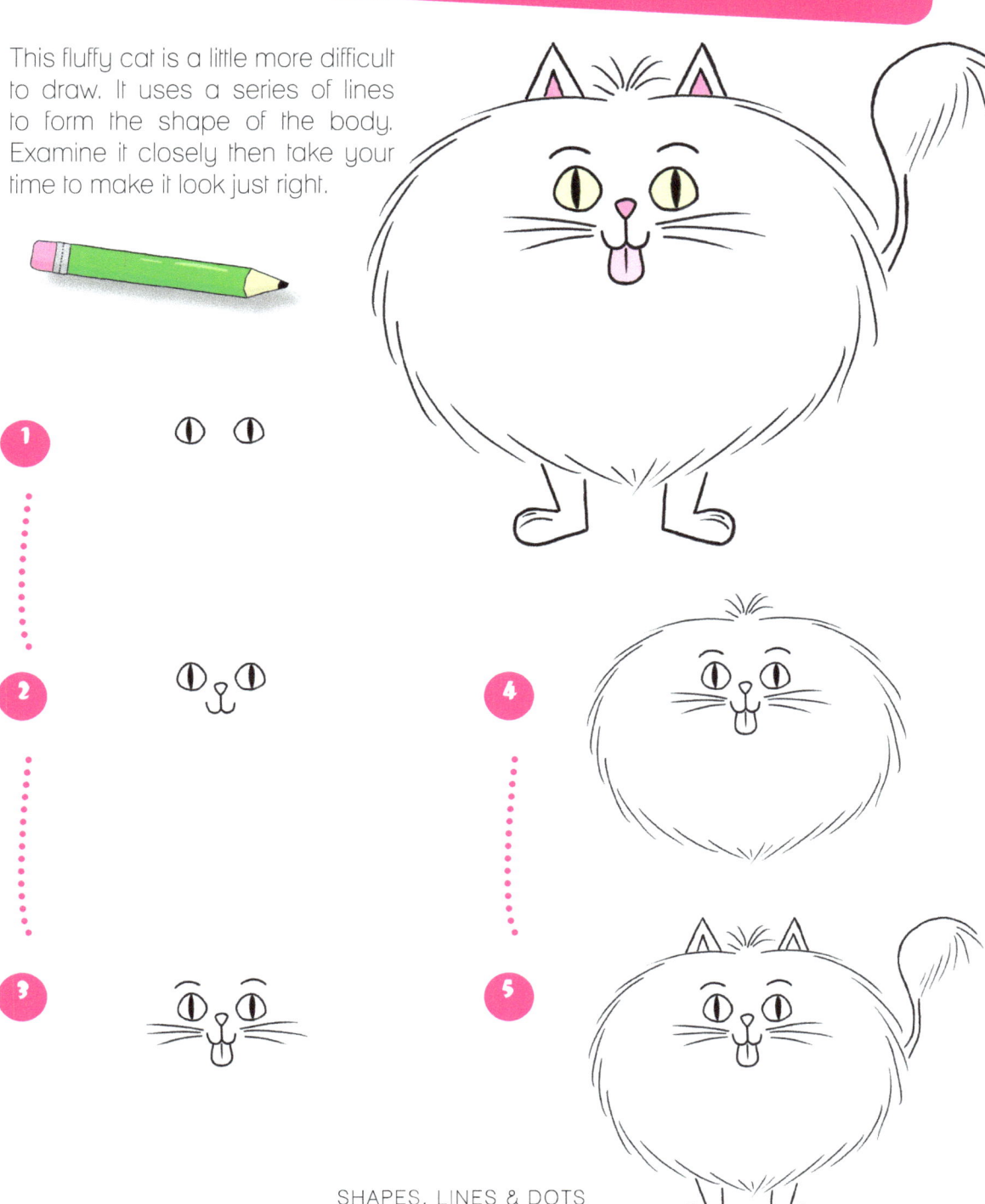

SHAPES, LINES & DOTS

Green Cat

Cats come in many colours — white, black, ginger, brown and grey. Some have spots and others have stripes. But you never ever see a green cat! Well, not until you draw a cartoon one at least. Use shapes, lines and dots to draw a green cat.

SHAPES, LINES & DOTS

Lion

The King of all the cats is the Lion! Ferocious and grumpy, always looking for the next tasty piece of meat. The cool thing is, lions are quite easy to draw. Follow the steps and construct your lion using shapes, lines and dots.

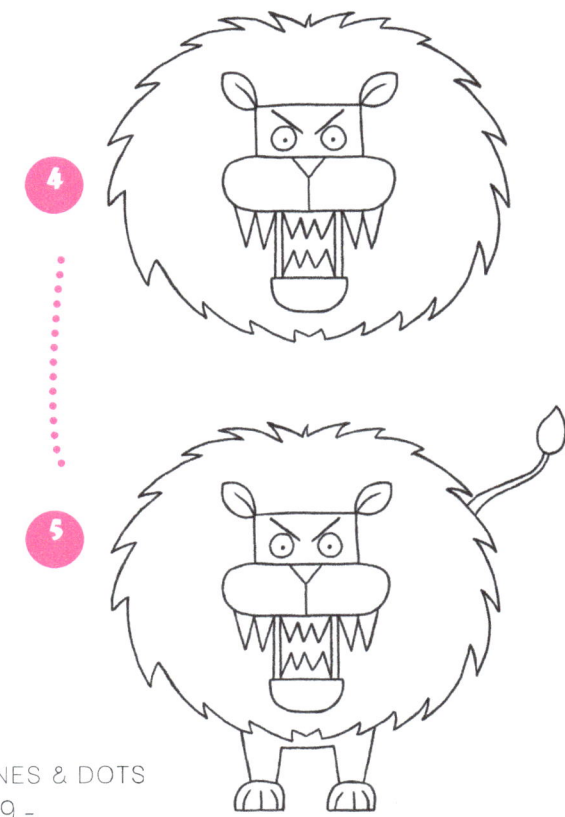

SHAPES, LINES & DOTS

Extra Activities

Try some of these cat drawing activities!

1. Do you have a cat? If you do, see if you can draw a picture of your cat and make it walk on two legs.

2. Draw the fat cat again, but this time make him a different colour.

3. There is one more cat in another section of this book. See if you can find it and draw it next to the cats from this section.

4. Cats like to chase mice. Using shapes, lines and dots, see if you can draw a cat chasing a mouse.

5. Take some paper or a sketchbook outside and choose your favourite tree. Draw the tree and then draw a cat fast asleep on one of its branches.

Dogs

Dogs have been called a human's best friend. They are fun and friendly, they like to play and sometimes they even have jobs! They work with the police, on farms, at the airport, in hospitals and with people who can't see very well.

There are about 340 different types of dog kept as pets, but the most popular by far is the Labrador.

I'm not sure how good the dogs we are about to draw would be as pets, but they certainly make fun cartoons!

Let's use shapes, lines and dots to draw some canine characters!

SHAPES, LINES & DOTS

Old Dog

This old dog has been a faithful companion for many years. He doesn't run much anymore, but likes to gently stroll through the park and take naps in the shade. Most of all, he likes a good belly scratch!

SHAPES, LINES & DOTS

Puppy

Just like baby humans, puppies have no teeth when they are born. They also can't see, hear or smell very well, and have to be looked after very closely by their Mum. Use shapes, lines and dots to draw this cute little puppy.

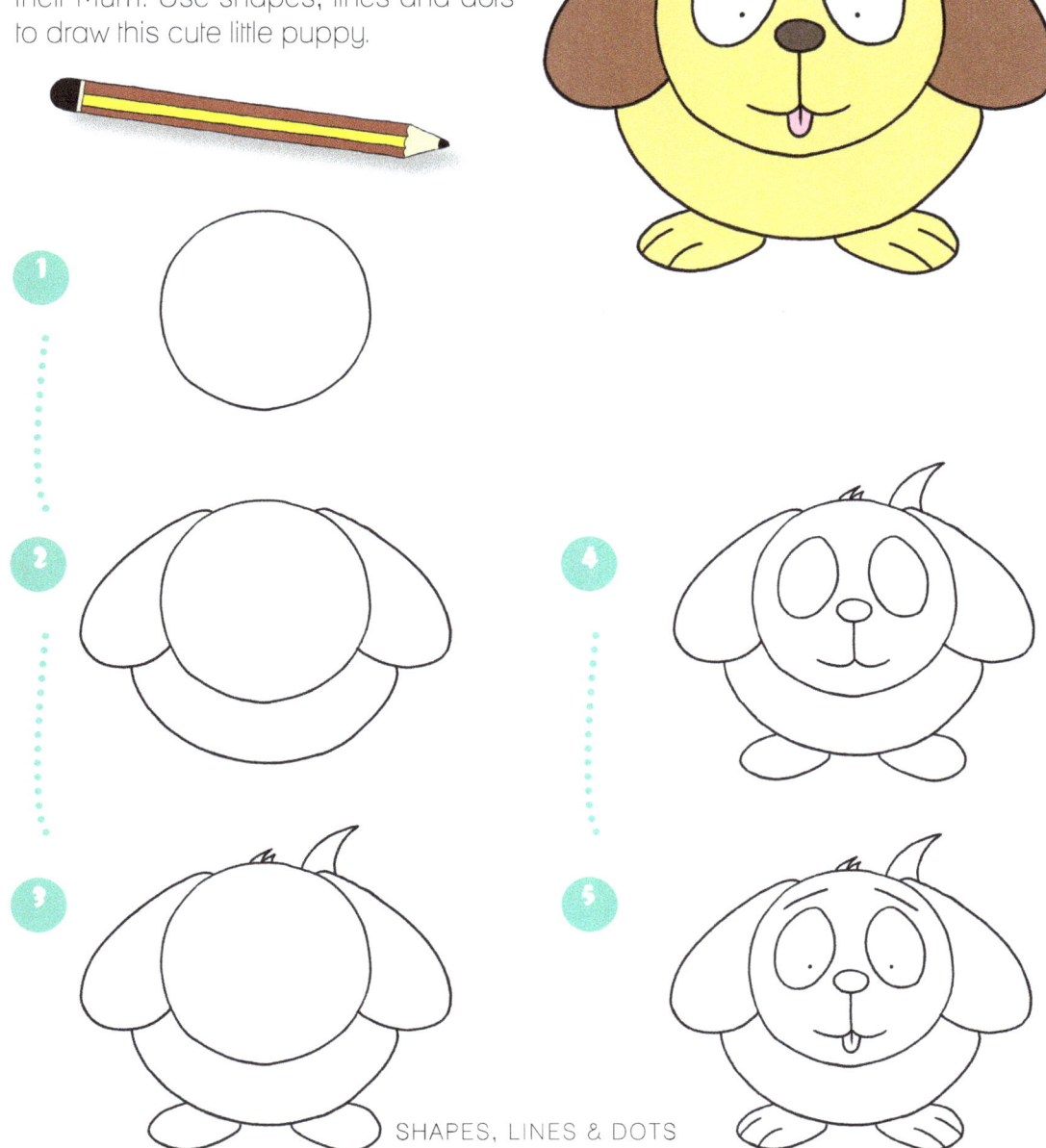

SHAPES, LINES & DOTS

Brown Dog

This brown dog looks a little sad. With droopy eyes and droopy ears, she always looks down. But look at the wagging tail - she's actually very happy and can't wait to play!

SHAPES, LINES & DOTS

Farting Dog

Did you know that if you accidently feed a dog grapes it will fart more? That's because grapes cause a chemical reaction in the dog's belly that produce a really stinky gas. It's very funny, but doesn't smell nice at all! Follow the steps to draw a farting dog.

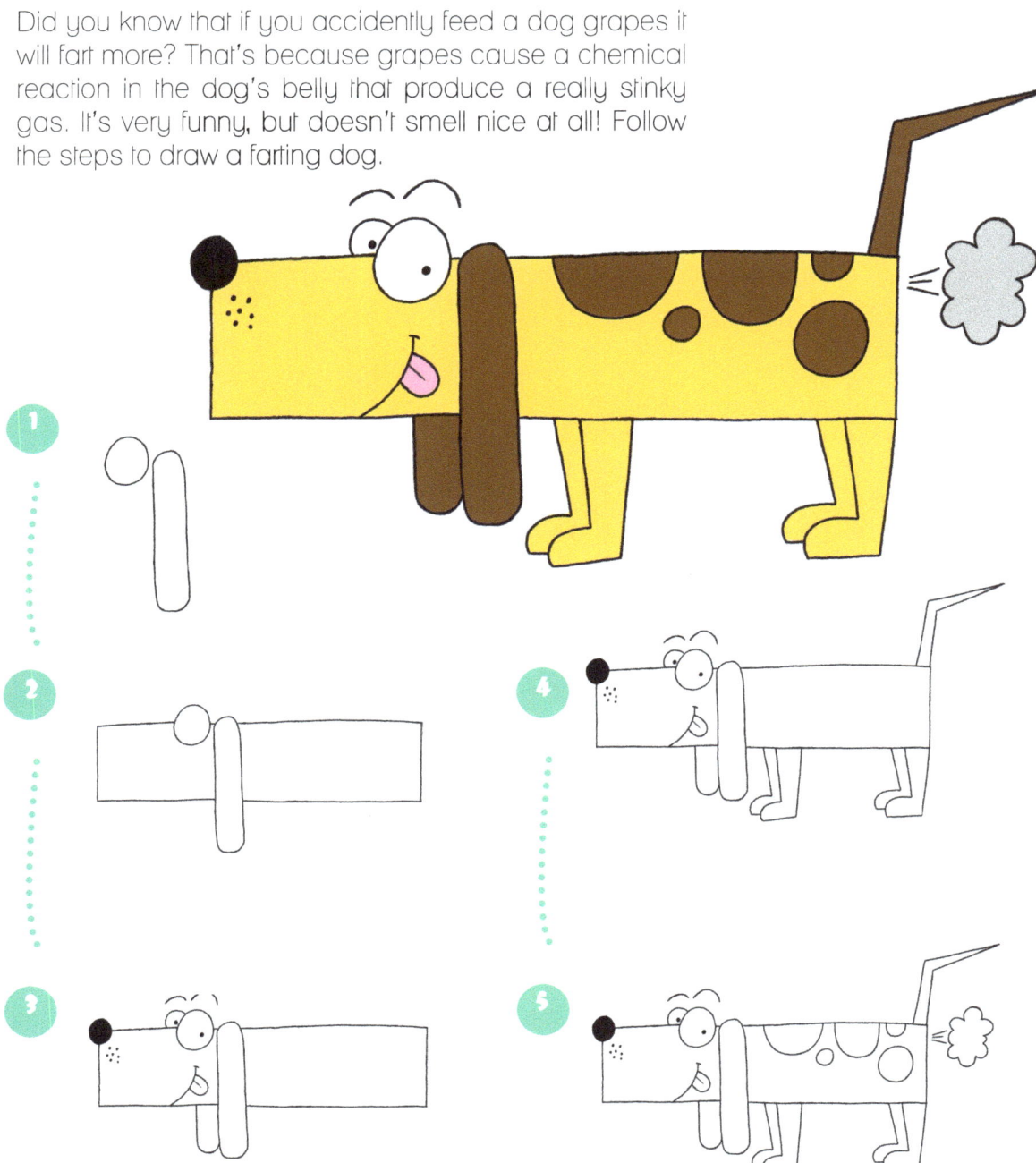

SHAPES, LINES & DOTS

Poodle

Poodles are funny looking dogs, particularly if the owner has dyed its hair and given it a strange haircut. I think if they had a choice, poodles would prefer to have dreadlocks – what do you think?.

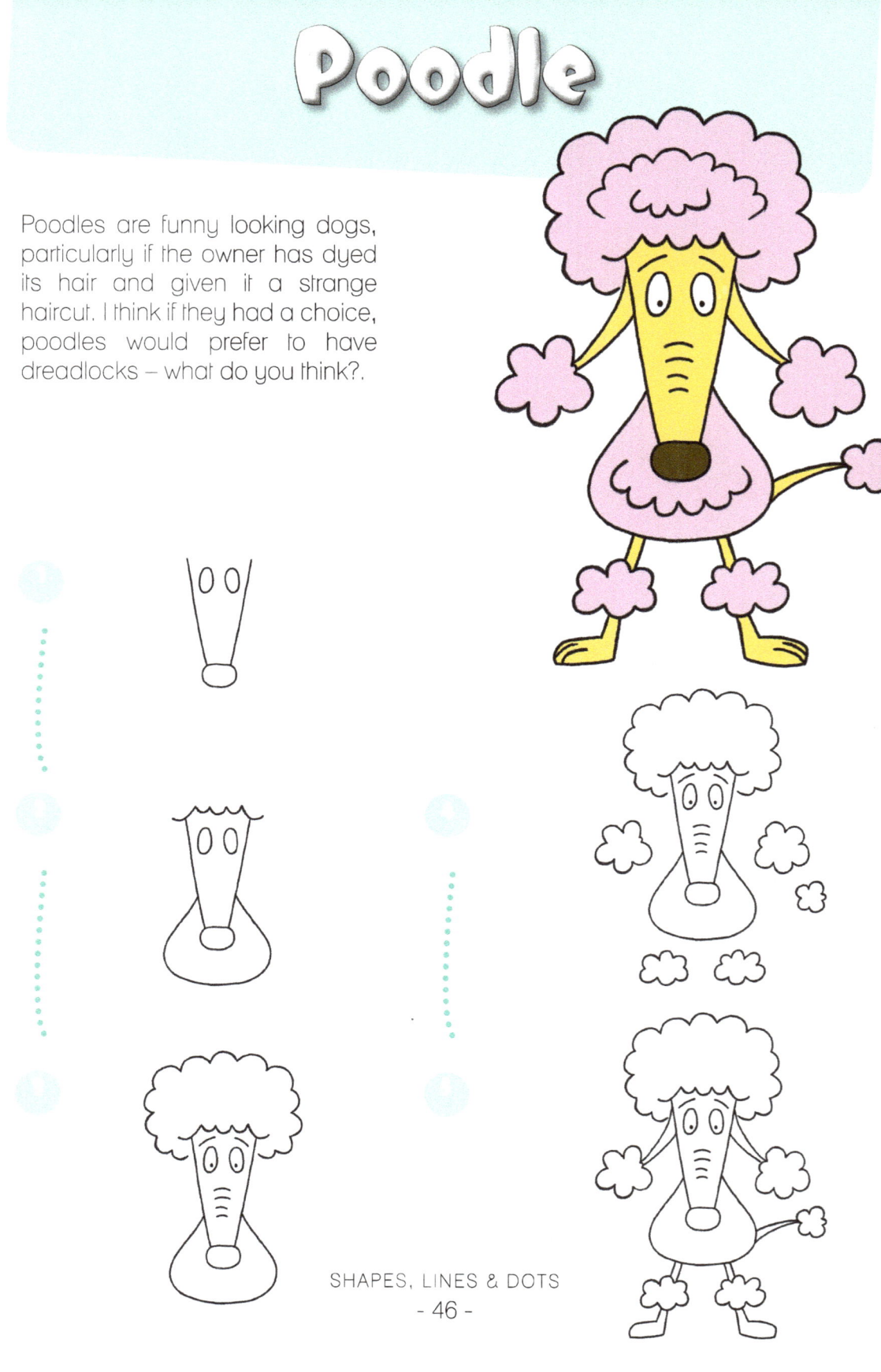

SHAPES, LINES & DOTS

Sheep Dog

Old English Sheep Dogs have been described as having a great sense of humour. Maybe it's because they keep laughing at all the poodles they see! Instead of shapes, we're using lots of lines to draw this fluffy friend.

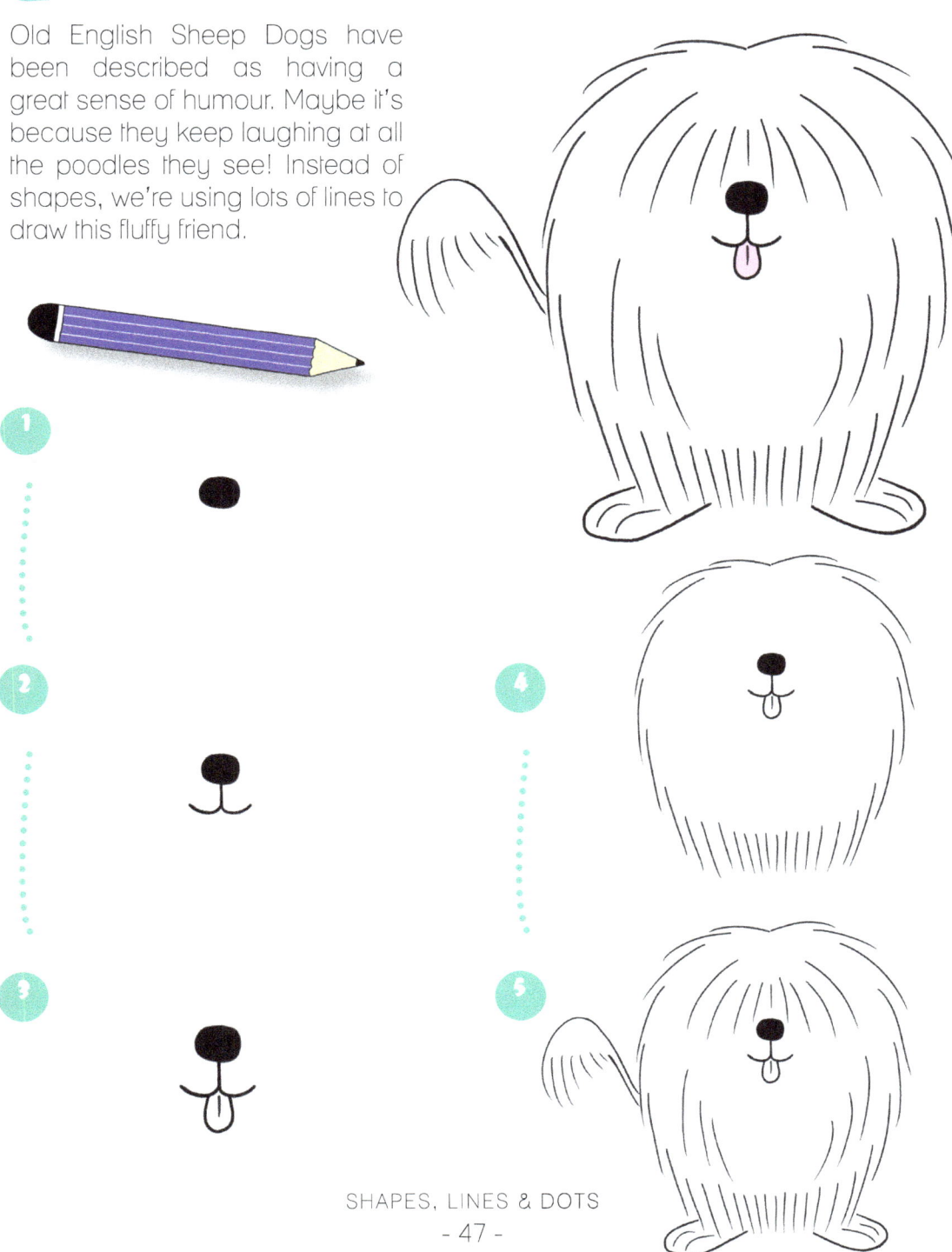

SHAPES, LINES & DOTS

Extra Activities

Have a go at these extra dog drawing activities.

1. Draw the poodle three more times. Colour each poodle a different colour – make them look ridiculously colourful!

2. Do you have a pet dog? Or does somebody in your street? See if you can draw it as a cartoon using shapes, lines and dots.

3. Sometimes you will see lots of people walking their dogs in the park. Take your paper or a sketchbook to your local park and draw cartoons of all the dogs you can see.

4. Draw a dog doing the most gigantic fart you've ever smelt!

5. Sometimes dogs dig holes in the garden to bury bones. See if you can draw a dog who is digging a hole. Make the garden look like your garden at home.

Sea Creatures

Most of our planet is covered by water. In the seas and oceans of the world, there are so many different creatures that it is almost impossible to count them all. Scientists guess that there are as many as nine million different creatures that live in the ocean!

Of course, there are lots and lots of fish, but there are plenty of other things that make the water their home. They are all cool to draw!

Let's use shapes, lines and dots to draw some cartoon sea creatures!

SHAPES, LINES & DOTS

Fish

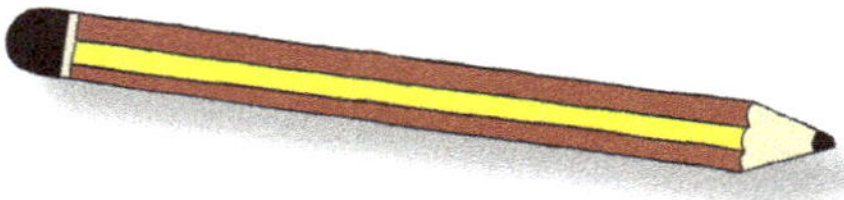

This is a beautiful pink fish. He lives in the coral of the Great Barrier Reef and is friends with lots of other colourful fish.

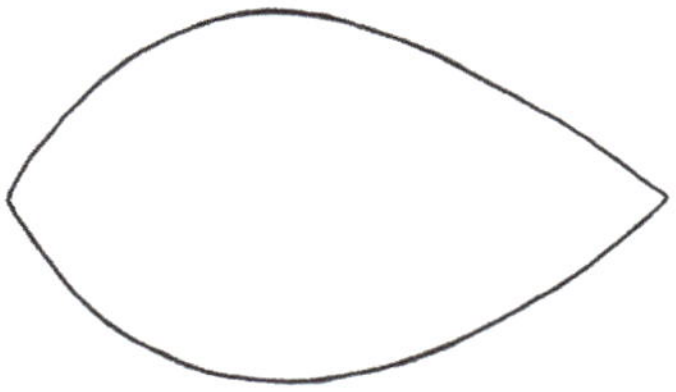

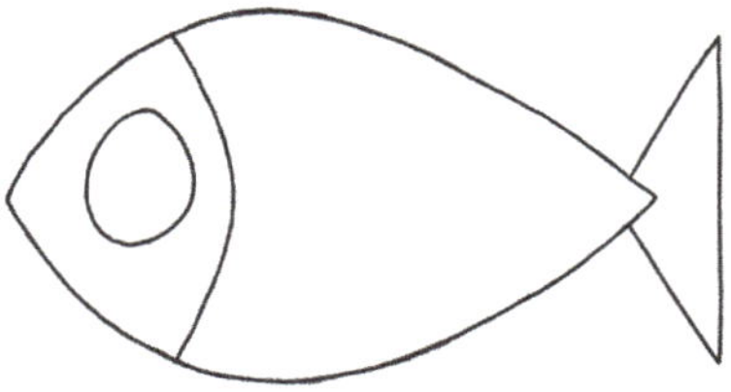

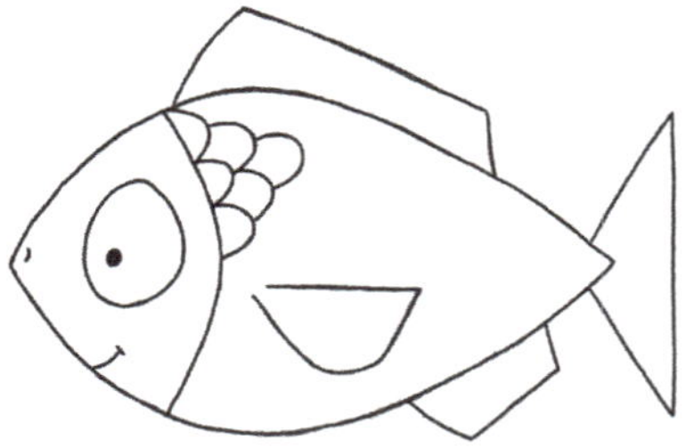

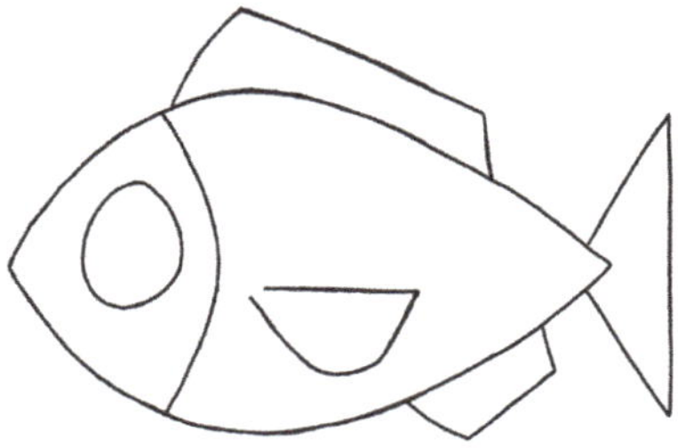

SHAPES, LINES & DOTS

Salmon

Salmon are unusual fish. They live in both freshwater and salt water, but when they move from one to the other, they change colour! Have a go at drawing this friendly looking salmon.

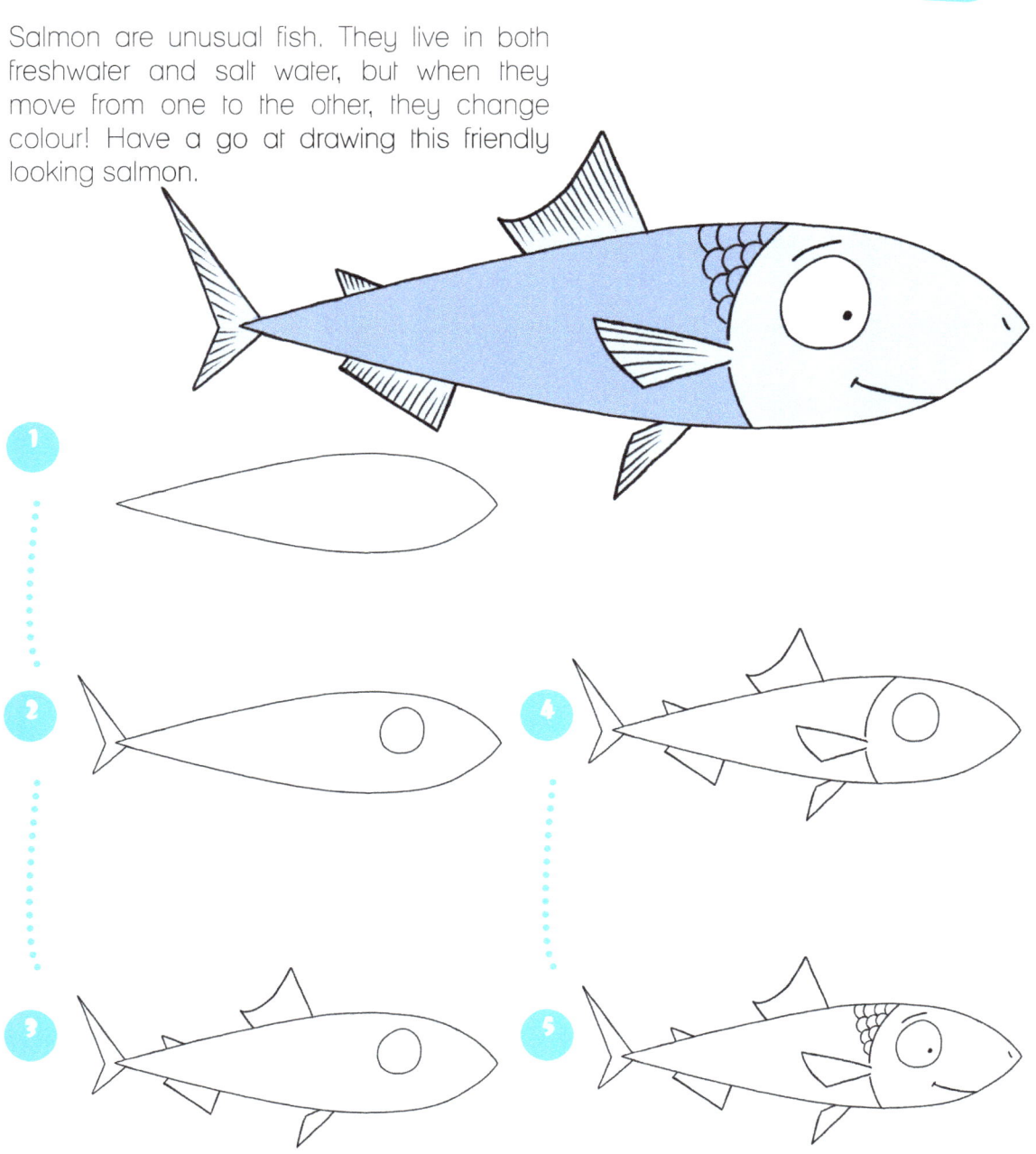

SHAPES, LINES & DOTS

Crab

Have you ever been nipped on the toe while exploring rock pools at the beach? There's a good chance it was one of these guys that nipped you. Crabs are amazing creatures and really fun to draw!

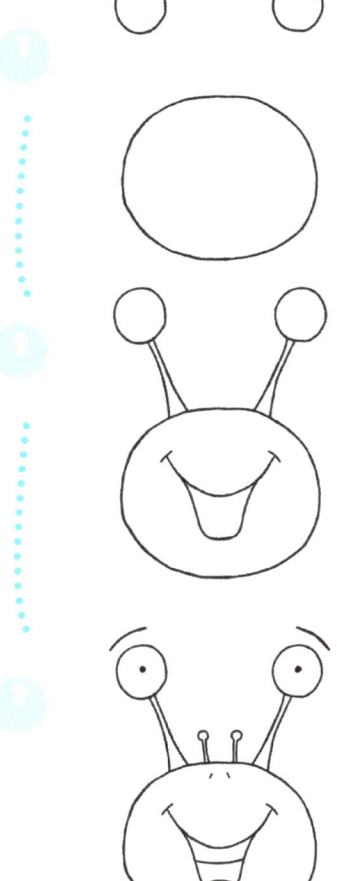

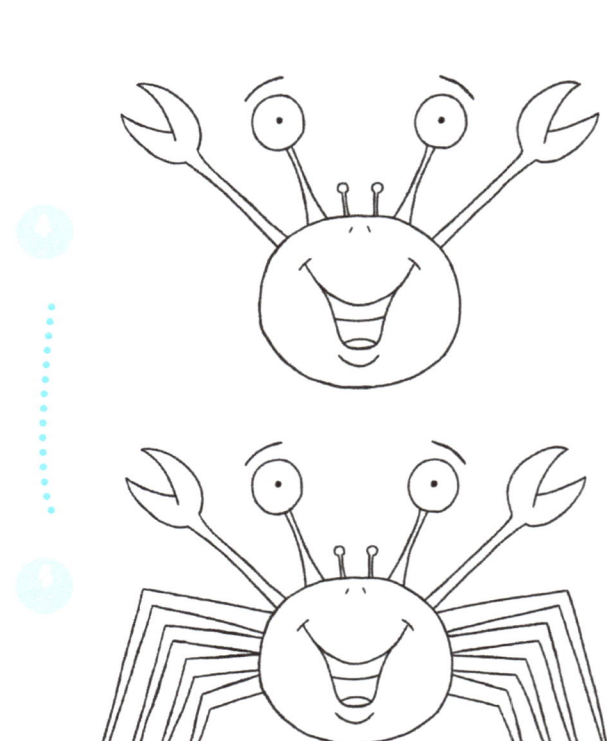

SHAPES, LINES & DOTS

Octopus

In Australia, the Blue Ringed Octopus is deadly. However, the purple spotted cartoon octopus is perfectly safe and fun to draw. The shapes in this one can be a little tricky, so take your time.

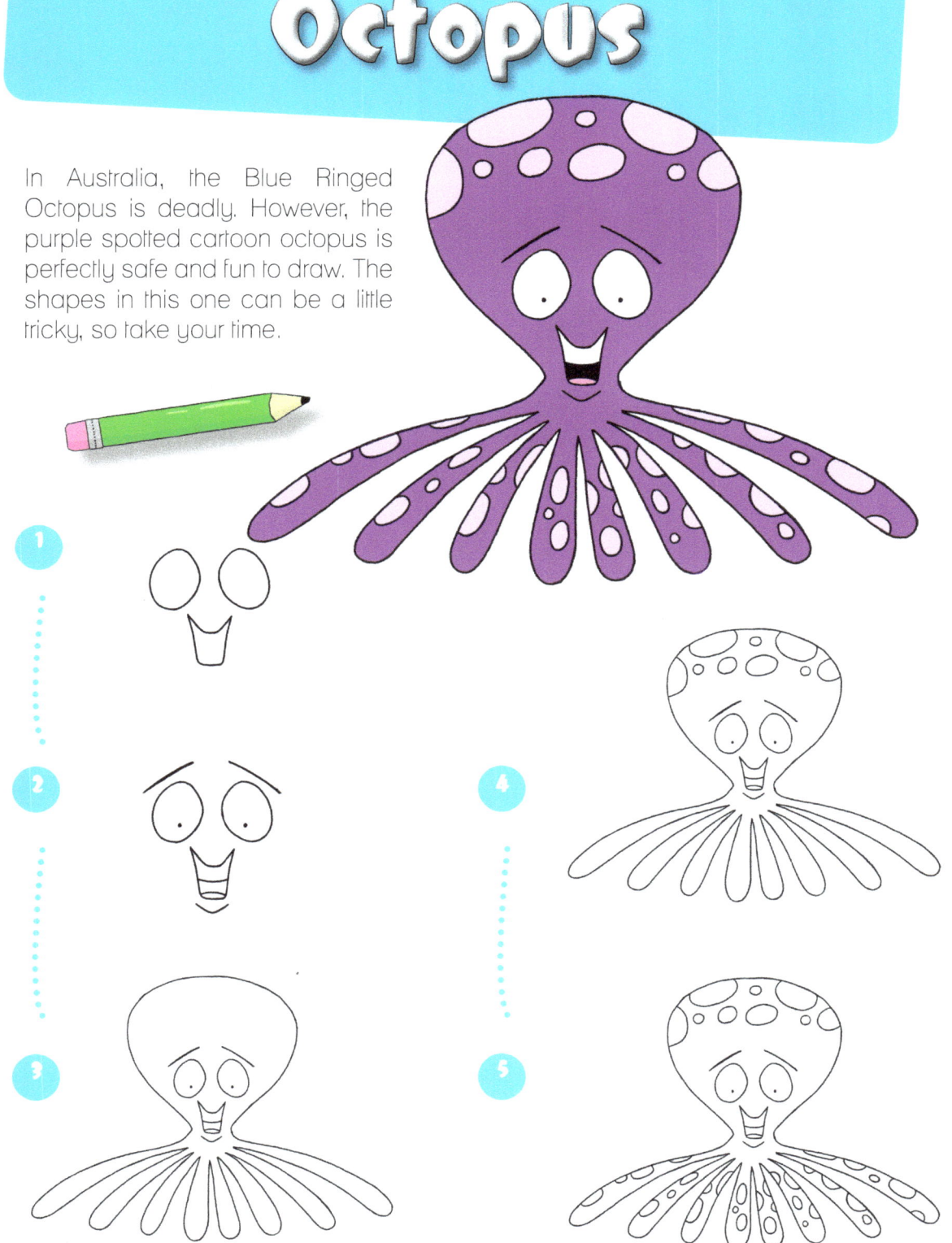

SHAPES, LINES & DOTS

Shark

The scariest of all sea creatures is the shark. Always grumpy. Always frowning. And always hungry! Follow the steps to draw this hungry shark and notice how the top and the bottom are different colours.

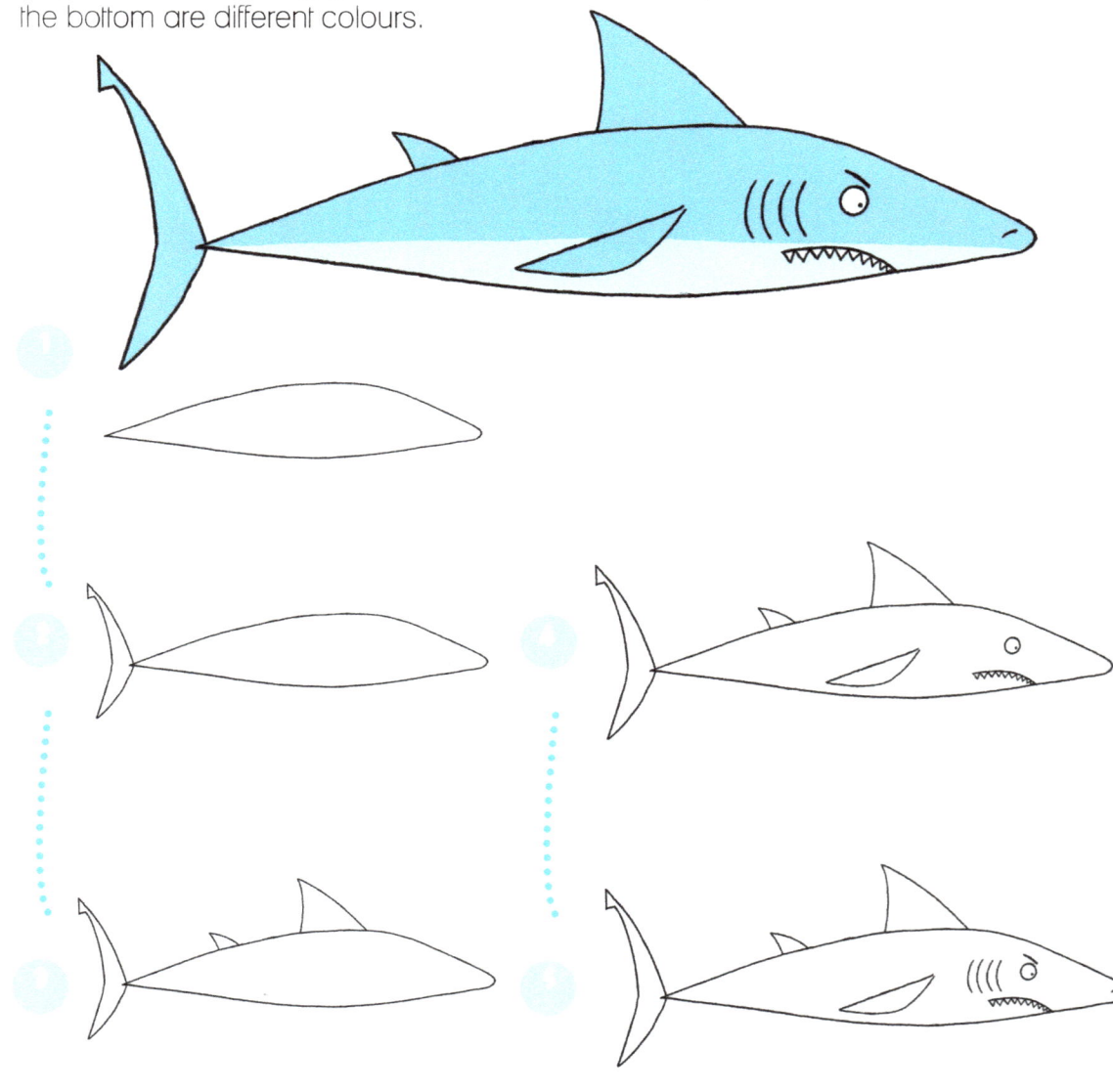

SHAPES, LINES & DOTS

Seal

From the scariest to the most playful - the seal! You might have seen seals at the Zoo or Aquarium doing all sorts of amazing tricks. They swim with incredible agility and speed. Best of all, they always seem to be happy!

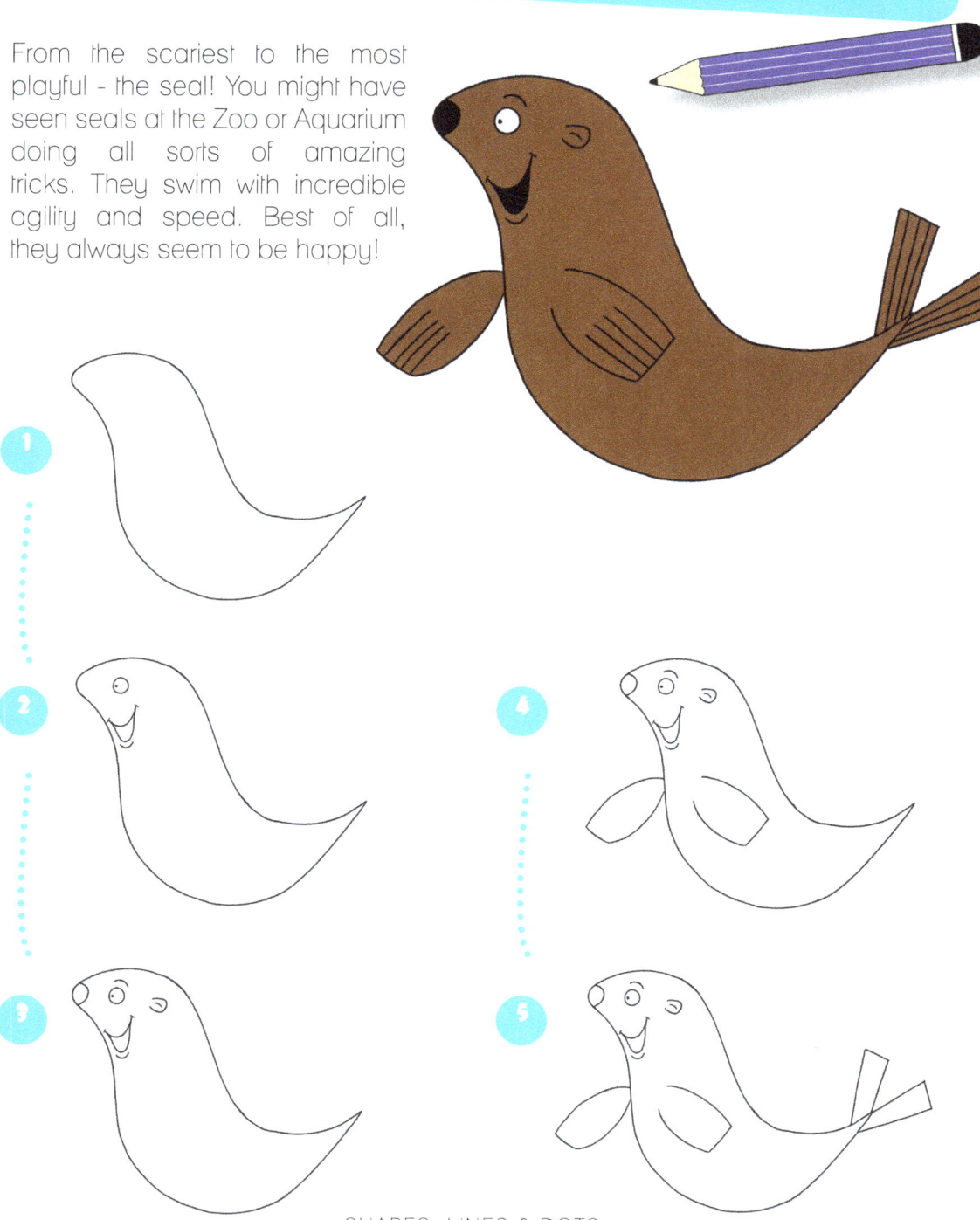

SHAPES, LINES & DOTS

Extra Activities

Try some of these extra drawing activities!

1. Next time you are at the beach, collect some shells. When you get home, draw them and turn them into cartoon creatures.

2. Jellyfish were almost too easy to even include in this book. All they are is a semicircle with some wavy lines hanging down. Draw some cartoon jellyfish.

3. Fish swim in schools. Draw as many fish as you can on one piece of paper and colour them all brightly.

4. Create an underwater scene for your cartoons. Using shapes, lines and dots, draw some rocks, some seaweed, and maybe even some pirate treasure!

5. Some fish can fly. Combining the things you have learnt about drawing birds and fish, see if you can draw a flying fish.

Farm Animals

I think spending time on a farm is something everybody should do. If you happen to live on a farm, make sure you invite some city friends to come and stay with you, so they can enjoy the clean country air mixed with the smell of cow poo.

There are over one hundred and thirty thousand farms in Australia, with most of them being run by families just like yours. Each farm produces enough food to feed about six hundred people for a year. We need to support our farmers because we wouldn't be able to eat without them.

Farm animals are all pretty friendly, but one can be a bit of a pest. Have your pencils ready and let's draw some farm animals using shapes, lines and dots!

Bull

Big and strong, but not very smart. Bulls usually cost a lot of money to buy, so farmers take good care of them. Did you know that all cattle are colour blind? Which means we can make them whatever colour we like and they'll never know!

SHAPES, LINES & DOTS

Pig

Pigs are very intelligent animals. They eat both meat and plants and there are about one billion of them in the world. That's a lot of bacon! Use shapes, lines and dots to draw a pig.

SHAPES, LINES & DOTS

Pony

Ponies are like small horses and are fun to ride. To look after them properly you need lots of space, so you could really only have one if you lived on a farm. But you can draw them anywhere! Carefully draw a pony by following these steps.

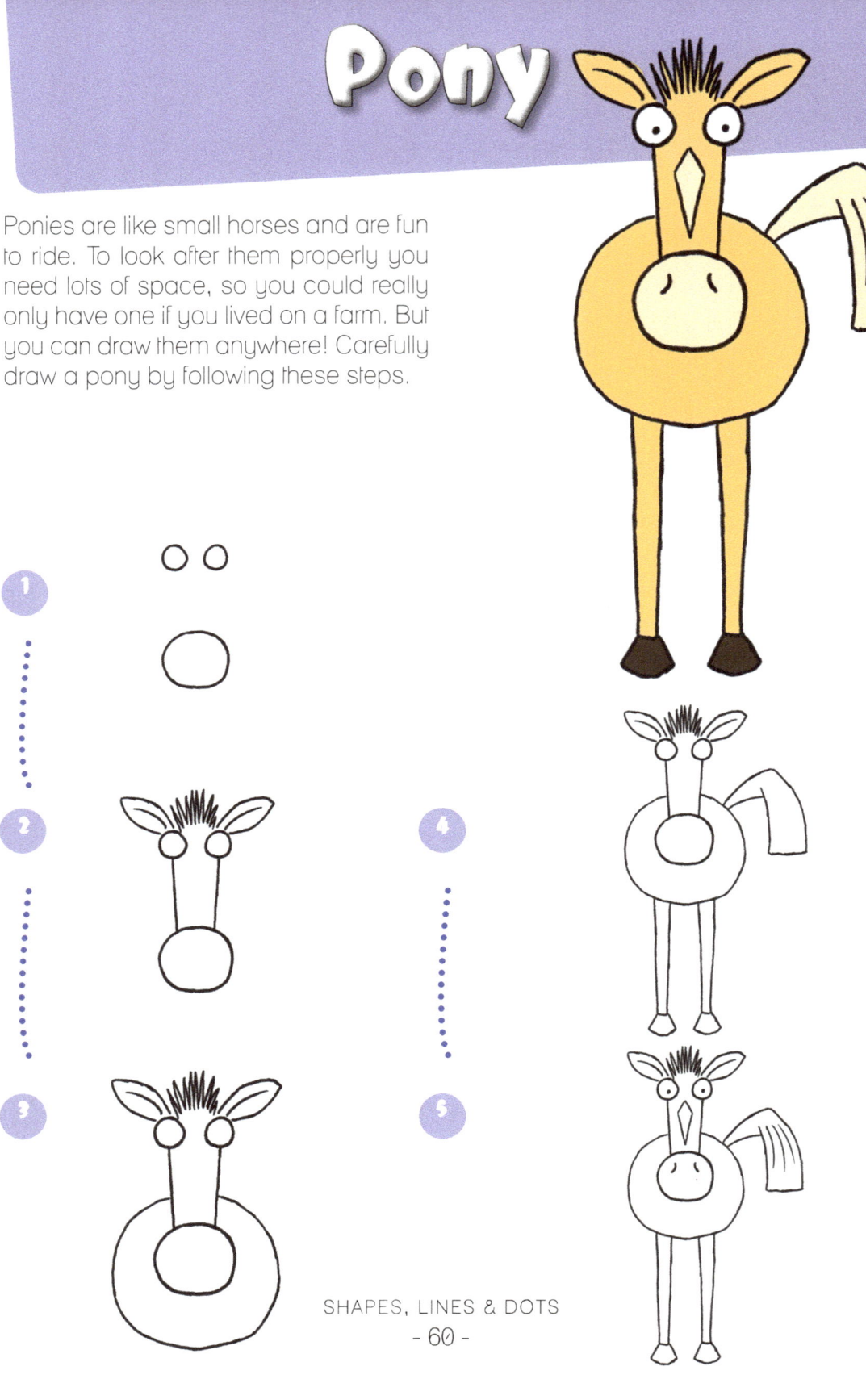

SHAPES, LINES & DOTS

Rabbit

Rabbits might be cute, but on the farm they are a pest, especially if the farm grows vegetables. But they do make great pets! If you're thinking of getting a rabbit as a pet, make sure you get two. They don't like to be alone.

1

2

3

4
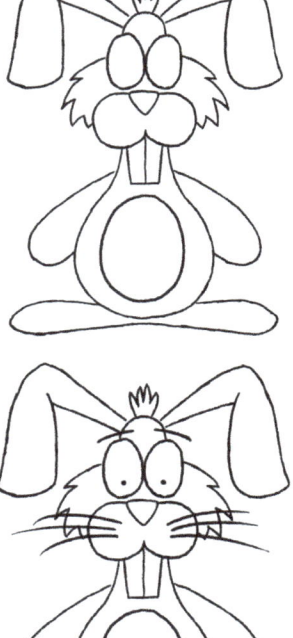

5

SHAPES, LINES & DOTS

Goat

Goats have excellent coordination. They have great balance and are able to survive in dangerous areas like steep mountains. They can even climb trees and some species can jump over two meters high.

SHAPES, LINES & DOTS
- 62 -

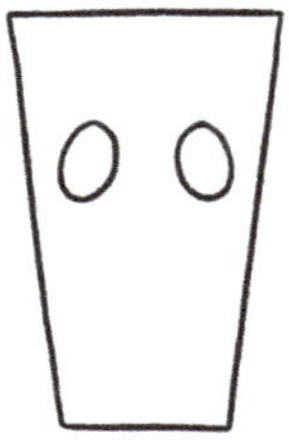

Sheep

Sheep are also intelligent animals, but they aren't quite as smart as pigs. They have great memories and can remember the faces of up to fifty other sheep! They also grow amazingly warm wool that we can make into clothes.

SHAPES, LINES & DOTS

- 63 -

Extra Activities

Try these extra cartoon farm animal exercises.

1. See if you can convince your parents to take you on a trip to a farm (if you don't live on one, that is) and take some photos of the animals you see. When you get home, draw some cartoons from your photographs.

2. Cattle come in all shapes and sizes. Some have horns and some don't. Some have spots and some don't. Some wear bells around their neck while others have tags in their ears. Using the bull as a guide, see if you can draw a herd of different types of cattle.

3. Draw a rabbit on a carrot farm stealing carrots.

4. With the help of a grown up, have a look inside your pantry or fridge to see which foods come from a farm. See if you can include those foods in a cartoon.

5. Near where I live, there is an Alpaca farm. See if you can find a picture of an Alpaca and turn it into a cartoon.

SHAPES, LINES & DOTS

Wild Animals

The coolest of all animals are the wild ones! The animals that you would find in places like the deserts of Africa, the jungles of Asia, or the outback of Australia. Animals with long necks, big bodies, horns, tusks and body armour. You can find it all among the wild animals of the world.

Sadly, many of the amazing animals that live in the wild are in danger of becoming extinct. That means they are dying and soon there will be none of them left. Unless, of course, we do something to help protect them.

We want all animals to have long and happy lives. And we want to be able to draw them as cartoons! Use shapes, lines and dots to draw these wild cartoon animals.

Hippopotamus

You might look at a Hippo and think it is slow and lazy. However, they can run faster than a human and are one of the most dangerous animals in Africa! Always be polite to a Hippo and never, ever, call them fat.

SHAPES, LINES & DOTS

Giraffe

Giraffes are the tallest mammal in the world. Even a baby giraffe is taller than most human beings. Long necks and long legs ensure they can reach the juiciest leaves on the highest branches.

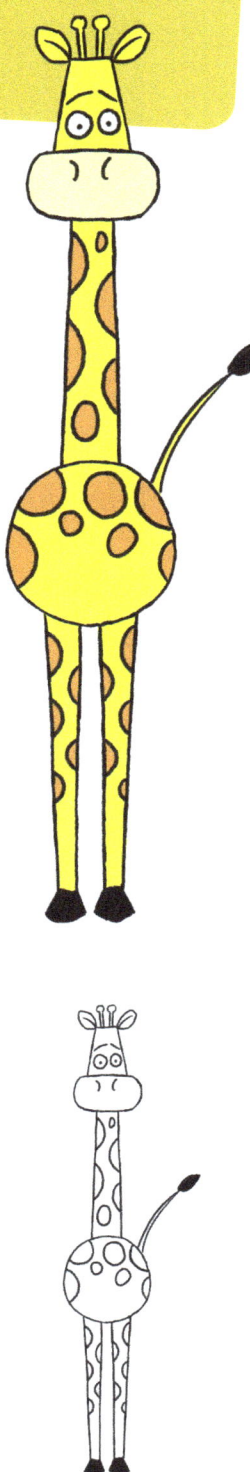

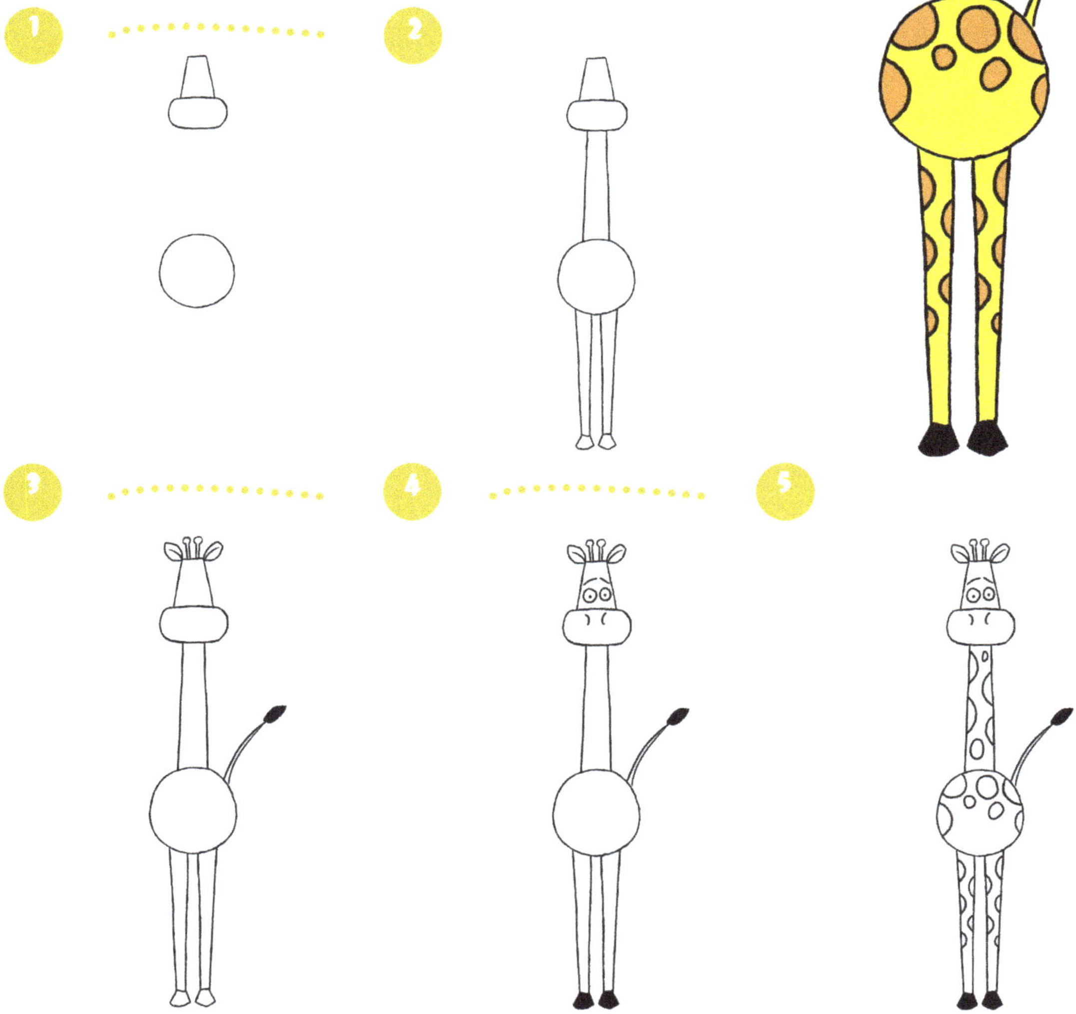

SHAPES, LINES & DOTS

Snake

There are about three thousand different types of snakes in the world. They eat meat, but don't have enough teeth to chew their food. So, they have to swallow their meals whole! Snakes have flexible jaws which means they can eat animals that are much bigger than they are.

SHAPES, LINES & DOTS

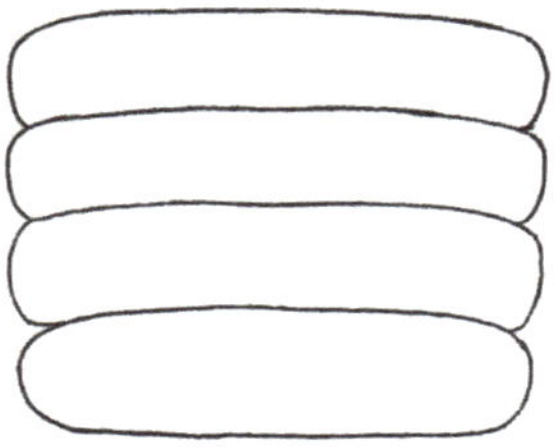

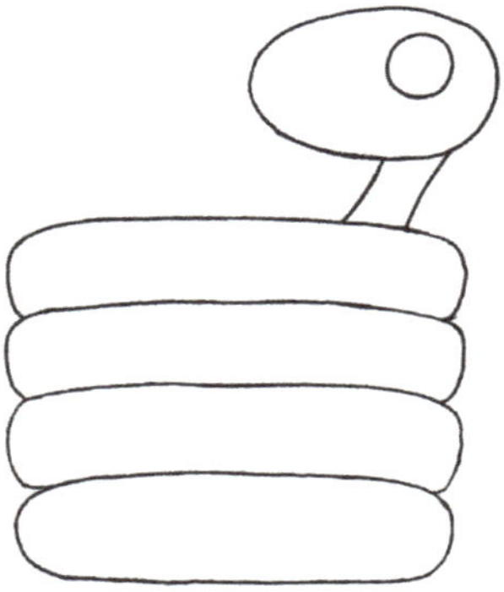

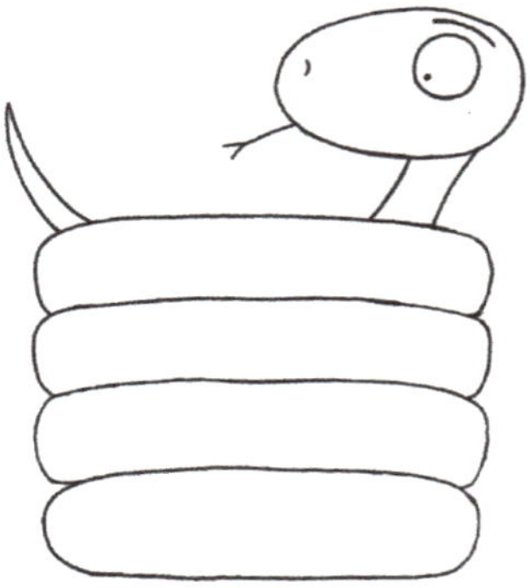

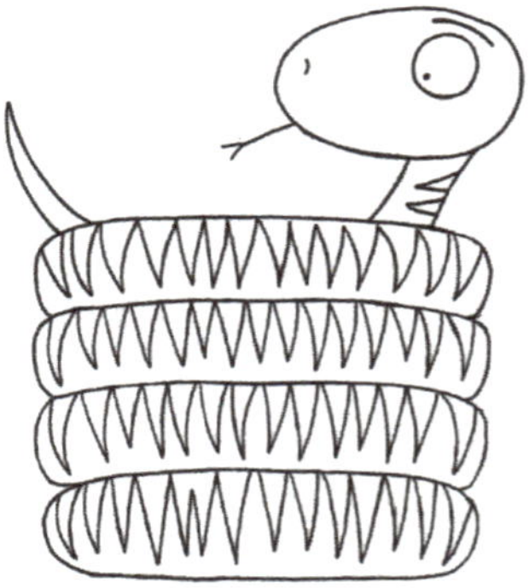

Warthog

Warthogs are ugly. They just are. They smell bad too. They like to travel in groups but instead of a simple name like a 'herd', or a 'pack', warthogs move around in 'sounders'. A weird name for a weird animal.

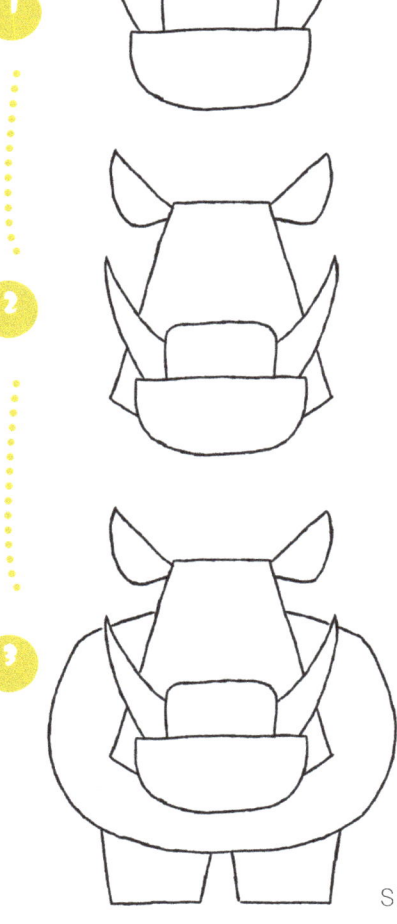

SHAPES, LINES & DOTS

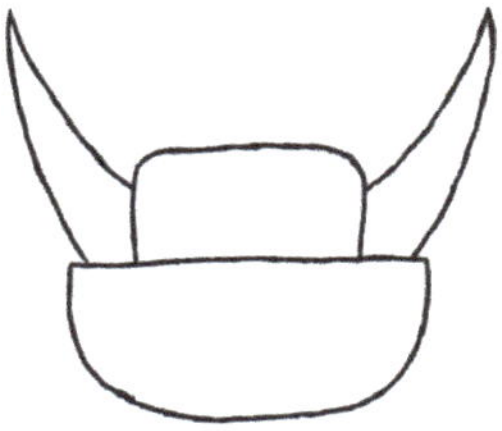

Rhinoceros

A Rhino's horn is made of keratin, which is the same stuff your finger nails and hair is made of. The name 'Rhinoceros' means 'nose horn' – I think you can see why!

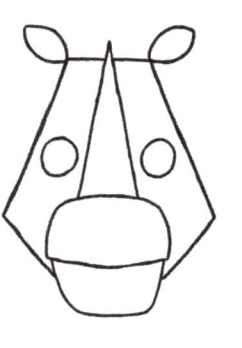

SHAPES, LINES & DOTS

Tiger

Tigers are the biggest cat on earth and are ferocious predators. They are very strong but can't run fast for very long. They use their stripes as camouflage and attack their prey by surprise. Follow the steps to draw a hungry tiger.

SHAPES, LINES & DOTS

Extra Activities

Try these extra cartoon wild animal exercises.

1. Hippos love to move around in herds. Often they'll go swimming together. Draw a herd of hippos swimming, with just their eyes and ears poking above the water.

2. Be on your best behaviour then ask your parents if you can go for a trip to the zoo or wildlife park. Take a sketchpad and draw cartoons of some of the stranger animals you see.

3. Spend some time in your garden and imagine you have a giraffe as a pet. How high would it reach? Draw a cartoon of a giraffe in your back yard.

4. Let's get the craft box out again. Instead of drawing a wild animal, see if you can make one with materials in your craft box.

5. This activity isn't cartoon related, but it is really important. Speak to your teacher at school and see if you can come up with a way your class can help protect an animal that is in danger of becoming extinct.

People

To finish our cartoon drawing adventure, let's draw the strangest, wackiest, weirdest creatures of all – people!!

People come in all shapes and sizes. We all have different ways of doing things, likes and dislikes, cultures and traditions. But deep down we are similar in that we all experience happiness, sadness, joy and despair. There's something unique and beautiful about being a person!

Cartoon people are fun to draw. We can give them big noses, small noses, or no noses at all. We can change their emotions by changing the way a line curves. We can make them anything we like.

I've chosen ten cartoon people for you to draw, but there are approximately a billion others you could choose from. Like with everything else, use shapes, lines and dots to draw some cartoon people.

SHAPES, LINES & DOTS

Curly Hair Lady

Some people spend lots of money to make their hair curly. But others have hair that is naturally curly – and they spend lots of money to make their hair straight! Have a go at drawing this curly haired woman.

SHAPES, LINES & DOTS

Bald Professor

In real life not all professors are bald. But they are in cartoon world! Follow the steps to draw a bald professor.

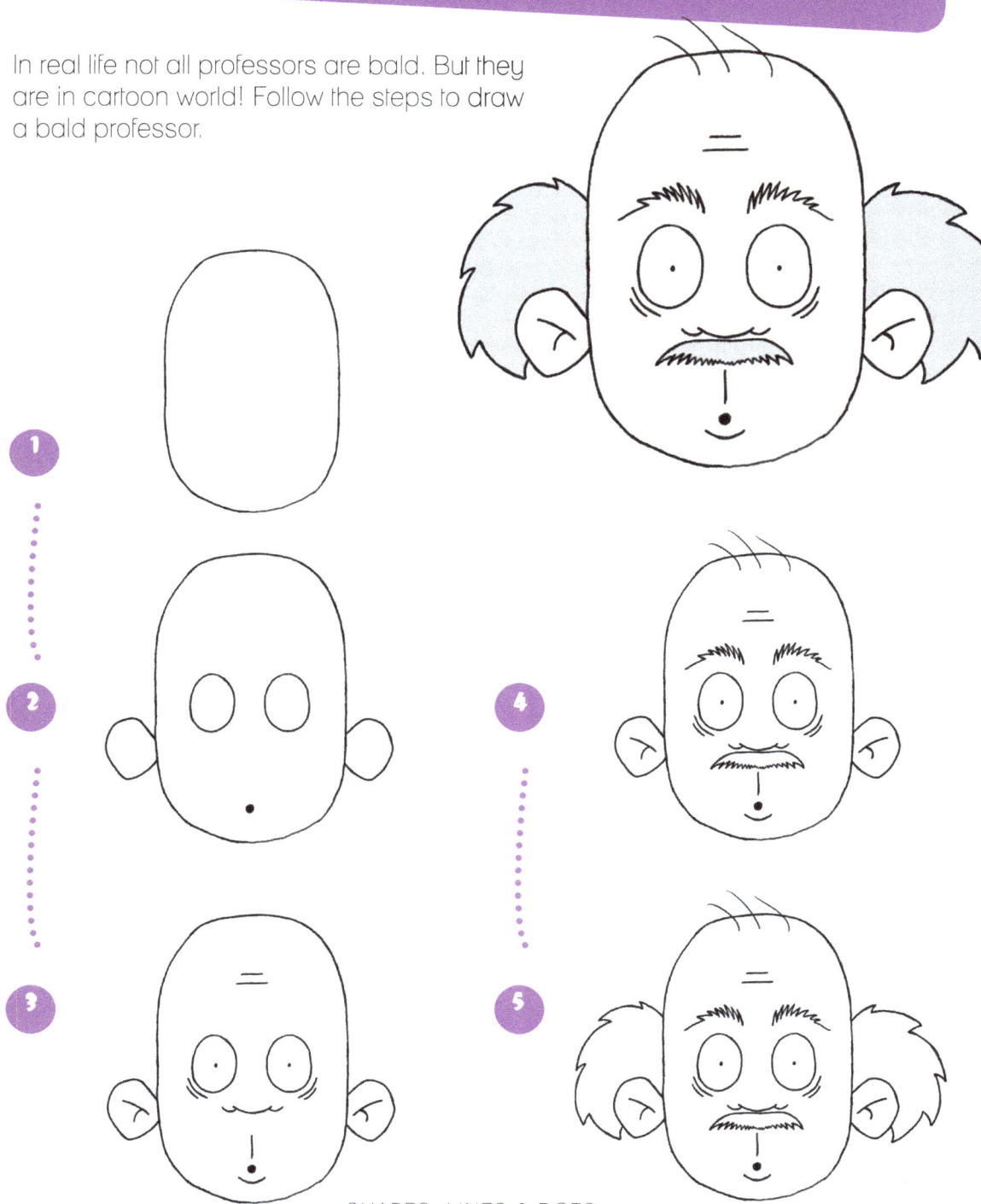

SHAPES, LINES & DOTS

Bearded Man

Did you know that the average man spends over three thousand hours shaving during his lifetime? That's a lot of wasted hours in front of the mirror! No wonder beards are becoming more popular!

SHAPES, LINES & DOTS

Blonde Girl

Blonde hair in adults is one of the rarer hair colours. But thanks to hair dye, blondes are in no danger of becoming extinct!

1.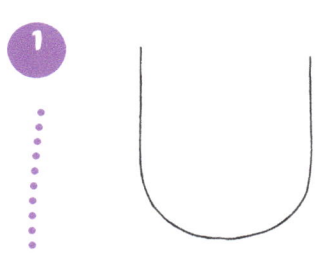
2.
3.
4.
5.

SHAPES, LINES & DOTS

Spikey Hair Guy

Have you ever been tempted to grow your hair spikey and dye it blue? Ask your parents if you can. Tell them Matt said it was ok!

SHAPES, LINES & DOTS

Cross Lady

This lady is not impressed. Maybe it was because we were having too much fun drawing cartoons? Maybe it's because we drew a farting dog? Who knows?

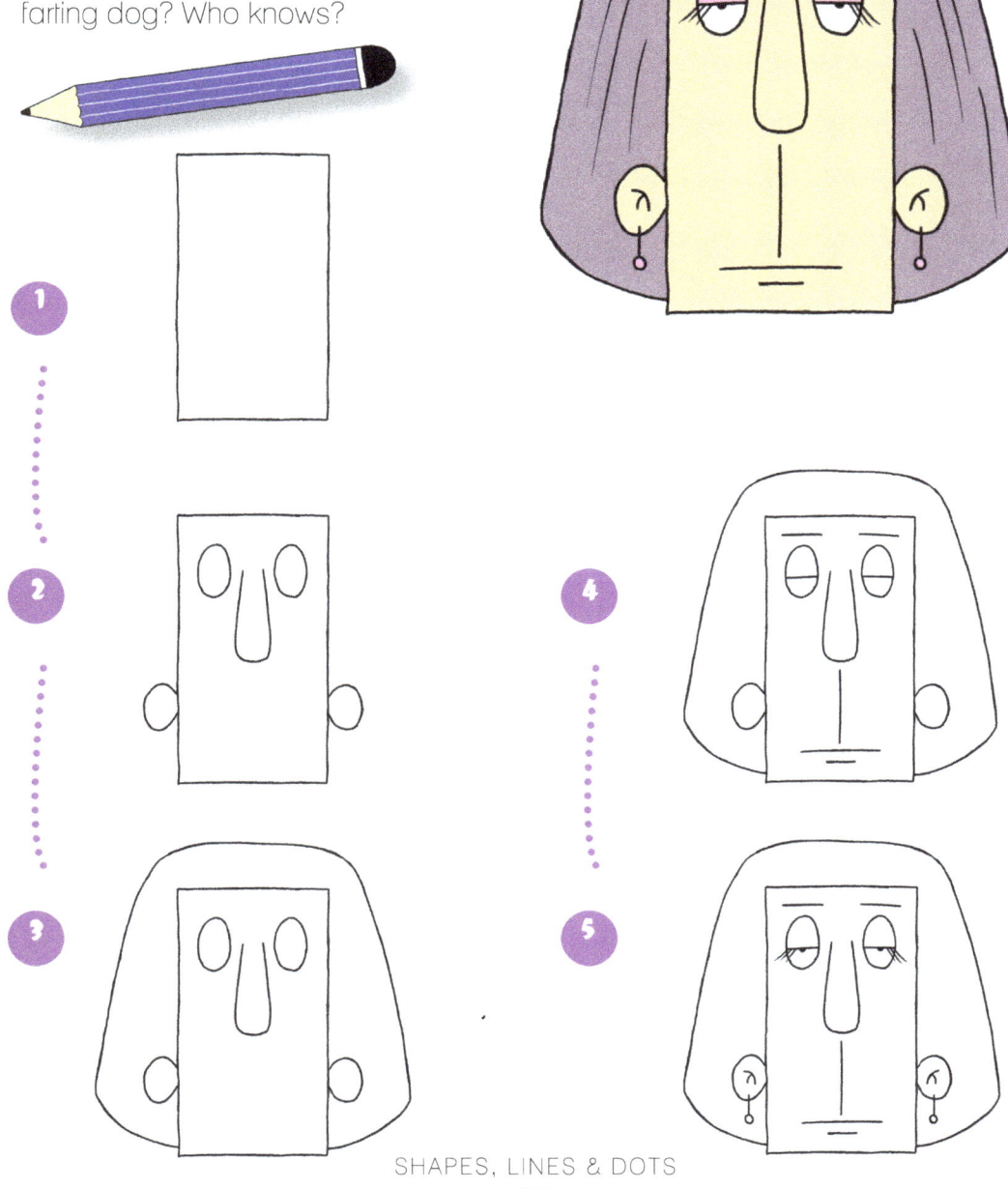

SHAPES, LINES & DOTS

Green Hat Guy

Hats have been around for as long as people have. The ancient Egyptians and ancient Greeks were the first to portray people wearing hats in their artwork. This guy LOVES his green hat.

SHAPES, LINES & DOTS

Old Lady

Old people are fun to draw. They've lived a long time. They know a lot of cool stories, and they have lots of character. All these things together mean that old people make great cartoons!

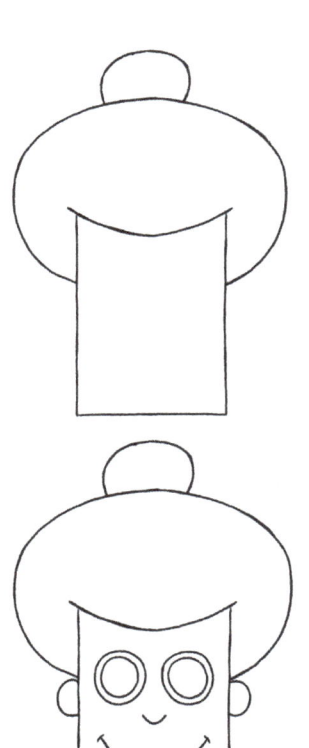

SHAPES, LINES & DOTS

Nerdy Guy

A cartoon world would not be complete without a cartoon nerd. Follow the steps to draw this nerdy guy. Then see if you can draw a nerdy girl.

SHAPES, LINES & DOTS

Crying Guy

All good things must come to an end. This guy is crying because he is the last cartoon we will draw together. That is, until my next book comes out…

SHAPES, LINES & DOTS

Extra Activities

Try some of these extra cartoon people activities.

1. Next time you are watching television, try and draw somebody from the screen as a cartoon.

2. Draw your teacher as a cartoon.

3. Draw your Mum and/or Dad as a cartoon.

4. Swap the gender of each of your cartoons. If you've drawn an old lady, try drawing an old man. If you've drawn a lady with curly hair, try drawing a man with curly hair, and so on.

5. Draw your brothers or sisters as cartoons.

6. Draw yourself as a cartoon!

7. Get your latest class photo from school. See if you can copy the photo, but this time as a cartoon.

8. Next time you have to go to a boring activity with your family, take your sketchbook and draw cartoons of the people that are there.

9. Make up a cartoon character all of your own.

10. Draw a cartoon person meeting one of the cartoon monsters from earlier in the book. Make them both look scared of each other!

Some Final Words

Thank you for sharing this cartoon drawing journey with me!

I started drawing when I was maybe four or five years old. My Dad taught me to draw and I've been drawing ever since.

I've had to practise a lot to get to where I am now, and I'll still need to practise a lot to get to where I want to be.

Drawing is my job, but I don't only draw because it is my work. I draw because it's fun and it brings me a lot of joy. Sometimes I draw because it makes me feel better when things aren't going well.

When I'm feeling stressed or a little bit down, I pull out my drawing stuff and draw. Just playing with shapes and lines and dots, putting them together in different ways, and seeing what happens, helps me see things differently, including some of the things that are bothering me.

So if you want to have some fun and get better at cartooning, pull out your drawing stuff! And if you ever find yourself in a time where things are not quite as good as you would like them to be, that's also a great time to pull out your drawing stuff. Do the drawings and activities in this book, or come up with something new of your own. You might never want to be a professional cartoonist, but it might help you feel a bit better. That's what drawing does for a lot of people.

If I'm ever visiting your school to run a cartooning workshop, make sure you come up to say hi. I'd love to meet you in person!

Until then, keep drawing!

Matt

Some Final Words

Matt has been a freelance cartoonist and illustrator for over twenty years. He is also the founder and director of MGA Counselling services, running two clinics in the Eastern suburbs of Melbourne. Combining his counselling and cartooning backgrounds, Matt runs a variety of creativity and wellbeing programs for children and adults:

- ☆ School cartoon incursions
- ☆ School holiday programs
- ☆ Birthday parties for all ages
- ☆ Corporate team-building activities
- ☆ Creativity and wellbeing workshops
- ☆ Summer and Winter "Scribble Schools" for kids

For more information on booking Matt for a cartoon, creativity or wellbeing event, visit **www.mattglover.com**

Some testimonials about Matt's cartoon drawing incursions in schools:

"Having Matt was fantastic! The children were so engaged. The material was really age appropriate and the children learnt so much about communicating feelings and emotions through artwork."

"The kids loved seeing 'real life' cartoons being created. Matt's approach and easy to follow instructions gave our students the confidence to have a go."

"Our students, and teachers, were hooked on what Matt was presenting!"

Buy the Series

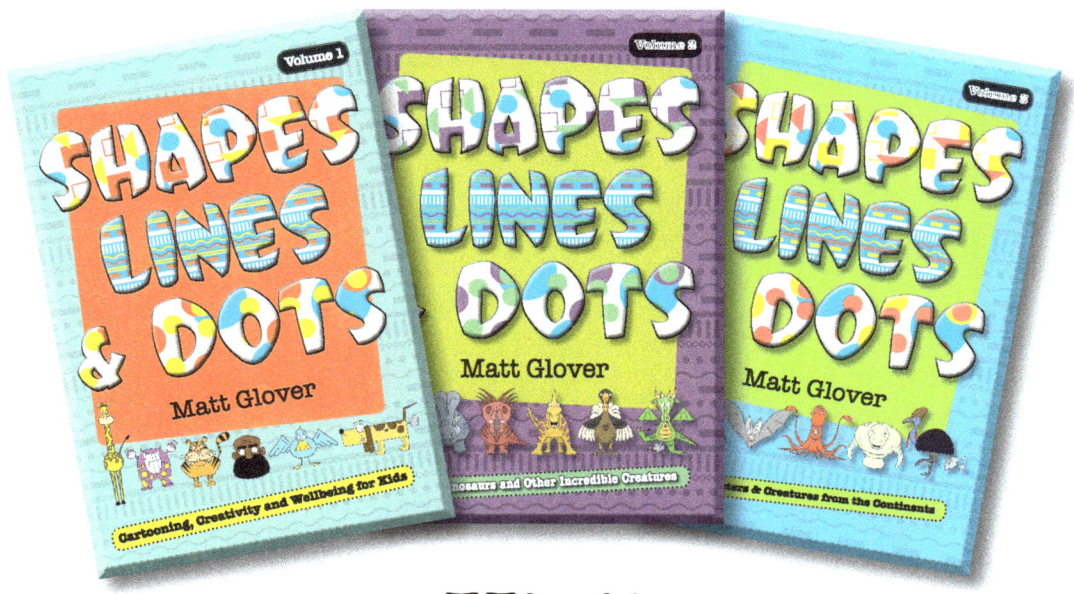

Visit
www.mattglover.com

for downloadable activities, updates on the latest volumes in the Shapes, Lines and Dots series, and to see a schedule of Matt's upcoming cartoon drawing workshops. Post your cartoon creations to social media with the hashtag #ShapesLinesDots

www.ingramcontent.com/pod-product-compliance
Lightning Source LLC
Chambersburg PA
CBHW061930290426
44113CB00024B/2861